V

In Praise of Idleness

'Invariably intelligent, stimulating and lucid.'

The Listener

'There is not a page which does not provoke argument of thought.'

The Times

Routledge Classics contains the very best of Routledge publishing over the past century or so, books that have, by popular consent, become established as classics in their field. Drawing on a fantastic heritage of innovative writing published by Routledge and its associated imprints, this series makes available in attractive, affordable form some of the most important works of modern times.

For a complete list of titles visit
www.routledgeclassics.com

Bertrand
Russell

In Praise of Idleness

And other essays

With a new preface by Anthony Gottlieb

With an introduction by Howard Woodhouse

 London and New York

First published 1935
by George Allen & Unwin Ltd, London

First published in Routledge Classics 2004
by Routledge
11 New Fetter Lane, London EC4P 4EE
29 West 35th Street, New York, NY 10001

Routledge is an imprint of the Taylor & Francis Group

© 1996 The Bertrand Russell Peace Foundation Ltd
Introduction © 1996 Howard Woodhouse
Preface to Routledge Classics edition © 2004 Anthony Gottlieb

Typeset in Joanna by RefineCatch Ltd, Bungay, Suffolk
Printed and bound in Great Britain by
TJ International Ltd, Padstow, Cornwall

British Library Cataloguing in Publication Data
A catalogue record for this book is available from the British Library

Library of Congress Cataloging in Publication Data
A Catalog record for this book has been requested

ISBN 0–415–32506–4

CONTENTS

Preface to the Routledge Classics Edition

John Maynard Keynes wrote that his friend Bertrand Russell 'held two ludicrously incompatible beliefs: on the one hand he believed that all the problems of the world stemmed from conducting human affairs in a most irrational way; on the other, that the solution was simple, since all we had to do was to behave rationally'. Russell was a better logician than Keynes, and could have objected that, strictly speaking, these beliefs are not incompatible at all. Keynes's point, though, is clear enough, and right on the mark. Russell exhibits a faith in the power of reason to solve problems that is belied by the examples of stupidity which he shows to have created those problems in the first place. If it is the lack of reason that gets man into his messes, how can reason get him out of them? For all his well-known hostility to orthodox religion, especially Christianity, Russell often spoke in the tones of an other-worldly prophet. The ideal of rationality may, like holiness, be almost impossibly hard to attain in this life; but it is the unshirkable duty of the prophet to laud it.

Russell looks down on human affairs from empyrean though not dispassionate heights. With a command of history that incessantly draws parallels with what has gone before, and a command of the natural and social sciences of his day that tries—sometimes less successfully, since scientific 'knowledge' quickly dates—to cast new light on old problems, Russell's prose delights by combining detachment and engaged, tart wit. The result can be shockingly blunt, or comically over-generalised. '[T]he peasant everywhere', he tells us in 'Modern Homogeneity' (pp. 130–7), is 'cruel, avaricious, conservative, and inefficient.' All peasants? Well, he is talking in terms of broad tendencies: of what the nature of peasanthood generally entails, given a certain conception of peasanthood. The opposite end of the social scale is treated no more kindly: 'The rulers of the world have always been stupid'. With such *obiter dicta* Russell is perhaps harking back to his Hegelian apprenticeship. Although his technical work in what has come to be known as analytical philosophy is rightly seen as a revolt against Hegel's overarching theories and iron laws of cosmic development, the Hegelian style of abstract generalisation still looms large, particularly in Russell's more popular writings on social topics. But the poetic licence of the entertainer is much in play, too. There are, he argues in 'The Case for Socialism' (pp. 81–106), too many hat shops in London, and they are 'usually kept by Russian countesses'.

When this collection was first published in 1935, a reviewer in the *Times Literary Supplement* wrote that because of his 'impatient' wittiness and lack of subtlety, Russell was a 'curiously unconvincing writer'. Yet the reviewer conceded that it is worth making an effort not to be immediately unconvinced, because 'the simplification of a problem, even the undue simplification of it, often means a new approach to it'. There is no better proof of this than the title essay of *In Praise of Idleness*.

Russell's theme and conclusion in this essay are startlingly provocative. Immense harm is caused, he argues, by the belief that work is virtuous, and only a 'foolish asceticism' makes us continue to insist on it in excessive quantities now that the need no longer exists. The First World War showed that the scientific organisation of production can keep people in fair comfort with a much smaller, or less active, workforce. For the well-to-do, Russell writes, it has long been acceptable for wives and daughters to be idle. Indeed, it has been positively encouraged. For the aristocracy it has been acceptable for all ages and both sexes to do nothing productive. Now we should recognise that, for everyone, 'the road to happiness and prosperity lies in an organised diminution of work'.

This cannot be called an unpopular view, because it is barely ever even considered today. Russell has not yet been hailed as a prophet for advocating it. But the time is ripe for that to change. Statisticians know that the amount of time spent on work has declined enormously and pretty much consistently throughout the twentieth century. Between 1870 and 1998, the number of annual hours worked per person employed has fallen by half in Britain. Since 1950 it has fallen by 24 per cent. Working people in rich countries have much more leisure than their grandparents had, but are barely aware of the trend, or of its implications when combined with other findings of social science. In 1998 in Western Europe workers produced, in real terms, nearly eighteen times what they had produced in 1870, while in the same period the number of hours worked per head of population fell steadily by almost half, from 1,295 hours per year to 657 hours. People have got vastly richer as they have spent less time on work, and differences between countries strongly suggest that longer hours do not automatically bring greater productivity—which implies that they could work fewer hours still and lose little. When France introduced a shorter working week of thirty-five hours in 2000, unemployment fell and economic growth remained strong, thus supporting the case for at least a little more idleness.

Perhaps more surprisingly, there is now overwhelming evidence that (above a certain minimum level of income) greater wealth does not bring greater happiness, either when two countries are compared with one another, or when one country is studied over time. This result holds good for all measures of happiness. While productivity per head in the developed world has swollen over the past fifty years, happiness seems actually to have declined. But none of this implies that you or I, or anyone else, might as well do much less work because we would be just as happy if we had more leisure and less money. On the contrary, surveys strongly suggest that, within a given society at a given time, the rich are happier. The solution to this apparent paradox lies in the fact that people, on the whole, want to be richer than their peers. It is relative wealth—keeping ahead of the Joneses—and not absolute wealth, that contributes to happiness. So if one person works less and earns less than others, this is likely to make him less content. But if everyone works less, and incomes fall in step, the result could be quite different. And more leisure for everyone is precisely what Russell advocated. On this, and many other topics, it would repay us to give him another hearing.

ANTHONY GOTTLIEB
30 MAY, 2003

INTRODUCTION

APRICOTS AND IDLENESS

I reread the essays in this volume while idling away my time in the garden of a friend who lives in the Loire Valley in France. In the garden stands an apricot tree, old and gnarled, riven with age, yielding less and less of its succulent fruit than but a few years ago. Its boughs still provide enough shade that I could read with pleasure Bertrand Russell's description, in the essay ' "Useless" Knowledge' originally published in 1935, of how peaches and apricots came to the west. They were first harvested in China during the Han dynasty, were then cultivated in India, moving eventually to what is now Iran, and finally to Rome. Moreover, he tells us, the etymology of 'apricot' can be traced to the Latin for 'precocious' because the fruit ripens early. The 'a', however, was added by mistake.

Russell (1872–1970) uses this example to show that knowledge can help the fruit taste sweeter by enhancing and enriching our experience with a sense of joy that might otherwise be absent. The 'mental delight' that I gained from reading Russell's paragraph while sitting in a French garden brought home his point quite vividly. The apricots were sweeter, the sunlight brighter, my appreciation heightened by the brief history of the fruit and its flawed etymology. This kind of knowledge, when valued for its own sake, can bring immense enjoyment to individuals even when it is as apparently trivial as the history of apricots. The 'contemplative habit of mind', which makes the pursuit of such knowledge possible, requires an idleness in which individuals become lighthearted, playful and able to engage in freely chosen activities, which are at the same time constructive and satisfying.

Russell believes that such opportunities for lightheartedness and play are particularly important in the education of the young, for without them children become listless, unhappy and destructive, their lives bereft of any appreciation for deeper, wider purposes. Ongoing opportunities for self-expression among the adult population are equally important because they allow individuals to appreciate the quality of their own experience, as well as the value of knowledge itself. Were it not for the idleness afforded by spending time under an *abricotier*, for example, I would not have appreciated Russell's argument for the intrinsic value of knowledge in such an immediate way.

For most people, even today, this kind of experience is not a realistic option open to them. They have neither the money nor the leisure time to idle away in the pursuit of 'useless' knowledge. They are caught in what Russell calls 'the cult of efficiency' where only the economic benefits of knowledge or the increase in power over others which these may bring, are valued. Those lucky enough to have the resources for idleness tend to spurn it in favour of the kind of 'vigorous action' that brings even greater control but little or no reflective understanding about the wider purposes of life. Russell regards this 'instrumental' view of knowledge as harmful because value is placed exclusively on its consequences rather than on the reasons underlying it. As a result, wealth and power are considered of the highest value, whereas idleness and contemplative knowledge are seen as so much loafing around.

Russell's proposed solution to this problem presupposes that idleness could now be made available to the general populace if work were restructured in ways made possible by modern methods of production. Not only is idleness a desirable state but it is one to which most people could accede if it were valued more highly than the busy, largely instrumental, activities that comprise the working day. Modern technology opens up the possibility of a four-hour working day becoming the norm with neither a concomitant loss in pay nor in the number of jobs. Russell suggests that men and women would then be free to pursue activities of their own making, liberated from the tyranny of work. Both working people and professionals could enjoy the kind of idleness to which only university professors, like myself, currently have access on their sabbatical year. Russell admits that some people would use their leisure time to make money and increase their power over others but their numbers would be balanced by those who engaged in more reflective activities (fishing, gardening and bowls come to mind), as well as a few who might even engage in various kinds of community work.

Russell's central point is that work, which he defines as moving bits of matter around at or near the surface of the earth, is not the aim of life. If it were, people would enjoy it. Yet, by and large, those who actually carry it out shun work whenever possible. It is only those who tell others what to do who laud its virtues. If idleness, play and the capacity to enjoy contemplative knowledge were valued in themselves, Russell's proposed reforms could be enacted. The purpose of In Praise of Idleness is to make the case for a world in which 'pleasurable, worthwhile and interesting' activities were freely pursued by all.

TOLERANCE OR UNREASON?

The book also reflects Russell's abiding concern for tolerance, peace and a balanced approach to individual freedom and social harmony. In the Preface he contrasts these with the unreason of bigotry, war and practical utility which tend to reign supreme. Less strident ways of resolving conflict are now needed, founded on 'calm consideration', 'a willingness to call dogmas in question' 'and a freedom of mind to do justice to the most diverse points of view'. Indeed, this 'general thesis binds the essays together', giving them a coherence shared by Russell's other social, political and educational writings.

The contemplative habit of mind enables individuals to consider all questions in a tentative and impartial manner for Russell, avoiding dogmatism of any kind and encouraging the expression of a wide diversity of views. Just as the scientific method enhances an open mindedness to fresh evidence on the part of mathematicians, physicists and philosophers in their attempt to reach truth, so the contemplative habit of mind can encourage ordinary citizens to tolerate the free expression of different points of view even when these conflict with their own.[1] For it is in the debate between these various perspectives that Russell believes conclusions can be reached which may be more inclusive and closer to the ideals of social justice. The apparently 'useless' approach to knowledge, founded on the contemplative habit of mind, thereby shows itself to be quite 'useful' in fostering social harmony.

Russell fears that the modern world's tendency towards an increase in the organisation of thought, coupled with its insatiability for unreflective action, undermines both the free expression of different views and the kind of tolerance for these views which he is seeking. In the essay 'Modern Homogeneity', Russell analyses the kinds of uniformity of opinion which he experienced during a visit to the United States in 1930. The level of homogeneity in thought and opinion, fostered by churches, the press, radio and cinema he found to be dangerously high. Professionals of all kinds, for example, were very much alike in their views simply because 'everybody was expected to conform to a pattern set by the successful executive'. He points out that the real dangers of this kind of social cohesion are an intolerance for minorities, an undermining of quality in favour of uniformity in every field, a 'somewhat blatant nationalism' and the risk of 'immobility', namely a stick-in-the-mud attitude resulting from a refusal to consider alternative viewpoints or courses of action. At the same time, Russell concedes that America's dynamism requires a considerable level of conformity and suggests that Europe is likely to move in the same direction: a warning that has a certain resonance today.

Two of the dogmas to which Russell is particularly averse are Fascism and Communism. They demonstrate the dangers of adopting extreme positions justified neither by empirical evidence nor by a full consideration of social justice. Moreover, they exemplify the most virulent forms of the tendency towards the organisation of thought in favour of obedient and strenuous action that have yet been devised. Of the two, Fascism is the more evil because its methods and goals are both inhumane. As Russell points out in 'Scylla and Charybdis, or Communism and Fascism', it is totally undemocratic, anti-Semitic and systematically deprives workers, Jews and other minorities of their rights. Despite the claims of its adherents, Fascism fails to resolve the problems of capitalist society.

Underlying these evils is Fascism's appeal to unreason and its constant valorisation of power. Russell analyses these characteristics in 'The Ancestry of Fascism' by tracing the intellectual roots of National Socialism to the 'Addresses to the German Nation' made by the philosopher Fichte in the early nineteenth century. Fichte claims that the purity of the German language makes it superior to all others, and calls for a national system of education which would 'mould the Germans into a corporate body' by attuning the individual will to that of the nation. These ideas were taken up in different ways by Mazzini in Italy, Carlyle and the Social Darwinists in England and Nietzsche once again in Germany. They took root in that country, however, because major industrialists and the military were both threatened by the Bolshevik regime, and managed to find support from large numbers of people from different social classes who felt dispossessed by rapid social reform. This unhappy combination of circumstances enabled the National Socialists to gain power: a fact which Russell views with prescient concern.

With regard to Communism, Russell finds himself in agreement with its end; namely, the creation of a classless society. But he cannot accept violent revolution as the means to bringing about such a society, for he believes it would produce tyranny rather than peace. This is partly because of his own evaluation of the Bolshevik revolution, following a visit to Russia in 1920, and also because of deeply held theoretical objections to Marxian theory, which he also lists in 'Scylla and Charybdis'.

Not surprisingly, Russell's own account of a saner, rational society, articulated in 'The Case for Socialism', is more moderate in its claims. In particular, he envisages a peaceful transition towards socialism, supported by a majority of citizens. He defines a socialist society as one in which there is both economic ownership of land, capital, minerals, etc. and a widespread democracy in all its institutions. By balancing these two key factors, he hopes to show that democratic Socialism is a viable alternative to both Communism and Fascism. He reiterates the need for a four-hour working day in order to bring about an idleness enjoyed by everyone. Indeed, Russell suggests that this reform could be enacted quite easily in a society where the wasteful production of weapons and the accompanying ideology of nationalism, or the 'cult of unreason', had been scrapped. Such a reform would appeal to professionals and the working class both of whom could feel at home in a democratic Socialist society.

Among Russell's other democratic proposals is a series of arguments for the emancipation of women, particularly working-class women, from the slavery of housework. While he applauds the fact that a growing number of professional women were finding employment outside the home in the 1930s, only socialist reform would enable working-class women to enjoy the same opportunities. In 'Architecture and Social Questions', he argues that the social isolation of working-class families in dingy, over-crowded and often unhealthy quarters hinders women from participating in social and economic life. Publicly funded apartment buildings in which a communal kitchen, dining room and leisure centre, as well as a sunlit quadrangle and nursery school, were provided would enable such women to work for a living and enjoy a certain leisure time away from their families.[2] Moreover, their children would be carefully looked after, well fed and given the freedom of movement necessary to lead healthy and inquiring lives. Russell seems to have in mind here the kind of school which he and Dora Russell ran for several years at Beacon Hill, with its ideals of 'fearless freedom' and peaceful co-operation. Although he came to think of the school as a failure, Russell did not abandon all of its ideals.

Indeed, education is a central concern of In Praise of Idleness. Radical educational reform is necessary if knowledge, learning and wisdom are to be valued for their own sake, and idleness, play and leisure to replace work as activities of worth. In 'Education and Discipline', for example, Russell provides a sketch of how education might look if it were based on these very different ideals. He suggests that teachers should work far less than they do at present, since any 'instinctive liking for children' which they might have is too often stifled by the demanding nature of the care they give. Two hours teaching a day is sufficient and should be coupled with another career that enables teachers to work and make social contacts away from the demands of children. This would enable them to maintain the 'affection' and 'spontaneous pleasure in the presence of children' required for a healthy pedagogical relationship. The far-reaching nature of Russell's proposal is shown by the fact that it has been taken up in recent years by teachers' associations in Canada, France and the United States.

In this new atmosphere, where 'a certain sympathy for the child's important desires' is once again possible for teachers, the right kind of balance can be achieved between their authority and the freedom of the child. Teachers' authority stems from a caring and tactful approach that enhances the growth of the child's impulses and guides him/her towards worthwhile intellectual and social activities. The freedom of the child, on the other hand, stems from those vital impulses without which no activity would be possible. In order to be led by these impulses in constructive ways, however, the child needs the mediating influence of self-discipline. S/he can then acquire the habits necessary for study, the achievement of long-term goals and the enhancement of the scope of his/her impulses. Like John Dewey (1859–1952) and Alfred North Whitehead (1861–1947), Russell believes that the only really effective kind of discipline is one that comes from within the child. At the same time, as he makes clear in 'Stoicism and Mental Health', the judicious use of authority by both teachers and parents is a crucial ingredient in the development of such self-discipline.

A child who grows up in this kind of atmosphere will learn to question what s/he is told in a disciplined and critical way. In 'The Modern Midas', for example, Russell argues that education should enable the public to question the judgements of experts about such important matters as the gold standard. By seeking answers that are founded on the evidence, a public which is educated in a self-disciplined manner will utilise the contemplative habit of mind to expose the shortcomings of conventional wisdom. In this manner, un-reason, masquerading as expertise, will be rooted out and challenged. As long as educational systems impede the ability of citizens to exercise such critical thought, 'one of the impediments to a successful democracy' will remain.

Finally, Russell challenges nationalism, as the major cause of the 'cult of unreason' both in schools and society by proposing an internationalism made possible by the establishment of a world government. Only then, he argues, could tolerance and international understanding really flourish. With regard to schools and universities, for example, all history texts would be vetted by a committee of internationally recognised historians to ensure that nationalist bias was removed. As an instrument of peace, world government would be produced by the conquest by one nation or group of nations of the entire world—a paradox to which Russell alludes in 'Western Civilisation' and which he develops in other works. Once a world government succeeded in gaining a monopoly of arms, war between nations could be stopped and peaceful coexistence ensured. In *Education and the Social Order* (1932) Russell admits that the price of such stability may well be the truncation of individual freedom for a very long time but asserts that this is a price worth paying for world peace. Possibly because this position so clearly undermines his commitment to free expression, Russell changes his mind in 'On Youthful Cynicism', suggesting that only when nationalist conflict has been curbed can civilisation flourish in the form of the search for truth and beauty.

Neither position takes into account the suffering involved in establishing and maintaining a world government of this kind. In his desire to extinguish the unreason of nationalism Russell espouses an unreason of his own. It is ironical that he might well have been describing the world that has emerged since the demise of the Soviet empire in which the United Nations acts as an instrument of the dominant Western powers. As I write these words (autumn 1995), for example, NATO war planes are bombing Bosnian Serb positions around Sarajevo and Cruise missiles are being launched from a United States warship. Meanwhile, neither peace nor inter-ethnic understanding seem any closer in the former Yugoslavia, for these actions have simply encouraged the Serbians and the Croats to launch their own offensives. While Russell might well have been critical of the actions of the Western powers, his own theory of world government, designed to eradicate the unreason of nationalism, lends itself for use in the justification of war.

WHAT KIND OF IDLENESS?

The frankly utopian nature of In Praise of Idleness is considered by some to be its main weakness. How, for example, could a four-hour working day be brought about without involving wage cuts? Since this is a necessary condition for bringing about universal idleness, one might expect some word on its instigation. This criticism misses the point of Russell's argument. He is simply suggesting that a world in which work was no longer the most valued of activities would be a much happier one. He explores the possibilities of a more leisured society in which the promise of greater idleness, held out by new technologies, was actually fulfilled. If one brings his definition of work up to date by including the movement of bits of information about the world, his argument recapitulates the stated purpose of the new computer and information technologies when they were first introduced to the workplace. They were supposed to make work easier and to bring greater leisure time to all. They are, however, now used to increase productivity by monitoring work levels and lengthening the working day. Instead of increasing the opportunities for idleness, these technologies have made more work for those who remain employed, while enforcing a desperate kind of idleness upon growing numbers of unemployed.

Productivity, measured in terms of efficiency and the bottom line, is becoming the sole criterion used to assess all work. Russell alerts us to the dangers of this view in 'In Praise of Idleness' as follows:

> The notion that the desirable activities are those that bring a profit has made everything topsy-turvy. (p. 12)

Put differently, we need values other than the profit motive by which to judge not only work but all human activity. A society, which fails to recognise the importance of an idleness freely engaged in, has turned its back on humanity.

Russell, of course, was not alone during the 1930s in writing of the importance of idleness. Karl Capek (1890–1938), the Czech playwright, essayist, philosopher and renowned anti-Fascist, published a short piece entitled 'In Praise of Idleness' in 1923 which was first translated into English in 1935, the same year that Russell's own book appeared. Capek distinguishes idleness from a number of other states with which it is often compared, including laziness, resting, wasting time, the 'mother of sin' and even enjoying a little relaxation. Rather, he considers idleness to be 'neither a pastime nor times extension' but 'the absence of everything by which a person is occupied' etc., a kind of 'standing still' whose rhythm he compares to motionless water, which 'gives life neither to weeds nor slime nor mosquitoes'. Idleness, however, does give rise to a sense of being in 'another world' where 'everything is a little alien and distant', an almost meditative state from which the individual emerges invigorated and ready 'to do something completely useless'.[3] Russell's contemplative habit of mind is somewhat different from this total withdrawal from the world that Capek describes because his notion of idleness is less of a negation of activity than a combination of leisure time with a playful contemplation. Nevertheless, both authors agree that 'useless knowledge' or 'something completely useless' is the aim of idleness and that more people should have the occasion to practise it.

Like Russell, Whitehead believes there to be far too little joy and spontaneous delight in the modern world. In education, the 'joy of discovery', which he calls 'romance', is too often stifled in schools and, while 'precision' is necessary, its duration should be short in order that 'generalisation', or the ability to relate abstract ideas to concrete facts, can flourish. Since the rhythm of education is cyclical in nature, romance re-emerges to ground generalisation in a more inclusive sense of joy, keeping it fresh and open to new possibilities. Whitehead clearly shares Russell's goal of encouraging a reflective idleness among students so that each individual can grow or achieve his/her fullest expression.[4]

For the same reasons Whitehead finds that corporations in the modern world kill the human spirit by negating two fundamental activities that are distinctive of any civilised society; namely, craftsmanship and aesthetic appreciation. Neither finds expression among producers or consumers because of an enveloping homogeneity brought about by factory production. The failure of corporations to encourage the free expression of such human activity results in 'a starvation of human impulses, a denial of opportunity, a limitation of beneficial activity'.[5] While he cannot bring himself to advocate a shorter working day, Whitehead clearly agrees with Russell's objections to the uniformities of work and opinion brought about by multinational corporations. Indeed, their views are far closer than is commonly supposed. This may be because the mutual influence, which both men experienced over a ten-year period during which they wrote *Principia Mathematica* (1910–12), did not cease upon its completion.

In any case, Russell wrote the fifteen essays in *In Praise of Idleness* by analysing the pressing social problems of the 1930s just as he had done those of the earlier years of the century, and as he would continue to do right up until his death. The clarity, wit and mastery of the English language which he brought to bear on everything he wrote, ensured that he was widely read, not only in Britain and Europe but also in the Americas, Africa and Asia. Indeed, these considerable qualities won him the Nobel Prize for Literature in 1951. It would be a mistake, however, to think of Russell as simply a fine stylist, for the ideas in these essays are important both for their own time and ours.

Howard Woodhouse
University of Saskatchewan

NOTES

1   Bertrand Russell, 'Philosophy and Politics' in *Unpopular Essays*, London, George Allen and Unwin, 1950, pp. 25, 27–8.
2   Russell acknowledges that considerable resistance to this idea would come from wage earners themselves but believes that women's determination to earn a living and gain more leisure time ensures their increased independence.
3   Karel Capek, 'In Praise of Idleness' in Peter Kussi (ed.) *Toward the Radical Center: A Karel Capek Reader*, Highland Park, NJ, Catbird Press, 1990, pp. 241–3.
4   Alfred North Whitehead, 'The Rhythm of Education' in *The Aims of Education*, New York, The Free Press, 1957, pp. 15–28. This essay was first published as a pamphlet in 1922.
5   Alfred North Whitehead, 'The Study of the Past' in A.H. Johnson (ed.) *Whitehead's American Essays in Social Philosophy*, New York, Harper and Brothers, 1959, p. 76. The essay was first published in *Harvard Business Review* in 1933.

Preface

This book contains essays on such aspects of social questions as tend to be ignored in the clash of politics. It emphasises the dangers of too much organisation in the realm of thought and too much strenuousness in action. It explains why I cannot agree with either Communism or Fascism, and wherein I dissent from what both have in common. It maintains that the importance of knowledge consists not only in its direct practical utility but also in the fact that it promotes a widely contemplative habit of mind; on this ground, utility is to be found in much of the knowledge that is nowadays labelled 'useless'. There is a discussion of the connection of architecture with various social questions, more particularly the welfare of young children and the position of women.

Passing further away from politics, the volume, after discussing the characteristics of Western civilisation and the chances of the human race being vanquished by insects, concludes with a discussion of the nature of the soul. The general thesis which binds the essays together is that the world is suffering from intolerance and bigotry, and from the belief that vigorous action is admirable even when misguided; whereas what is needed in our very complex modern society is calm consideration, with readiness to call dogmas in question and freedom of mind to do justice to the most diverse points of view.

Of the other essays in this volume, some are new, while others, which have been already published in magazines, are here reprinted by the kind permission of the editors. 'In Praise of Idleness' and 'The Modern Midas' appeared in *Harper's Magazine*; 'The Ancestry of Fascism' (under a different title) appeared in *The Political Quarterly* in England and *The Atlantic Monthly* in America; 'Scylla and Charybdis, or Communism and Fascism' appeared in *The Modern Monthly*; 'Modern Homogeneity' in New York in *The Outlook* (now *The New Outlook*); 'Education and Discipline' was published in *The New Statesman and Nation*. I have also to acknowledge the assistance of Peter Spence in suggesting and discussing many of the subjects.

1

IN PRAISE OF IDLENESS[1]

Like most of my generation, I was brought up on the saying: 'Satan finds some mischief still for idle hands to do.' Being a highly virtuous child, I believed all that I was told, and acquired a conscience which has kept me working hard down to the present moment. But although my conscience has controlled my *actions*, my *opinions* have undergone a revolution. I think that there is far too much work done in the world, that immense harm is caused by the belief that work is virtuous, and that what needs to be preached in modern industrial countries is quite different from what always has been preached. Everyone knows the story of the traveller in Naples who saw twelve beggars lying in the sun (it was before the days of Mussolini), and offered a lira to the laziest of them. Eleven of them jumped up to claim it, so he gave it to the twelfth. This traveller was on the right lines. But in countries which do not enjoy Mediterranean sunshine idleness is more difficult, and a great public propaganda will be required

[1] Written in 1932.

to inaugurate it. I hope that, after reading the following pages, the leaders of the YMCA will start a campaign to induce good young men to do nothing. If so, I shall not have lived in vain.

Before advancing my own arguments for laziness, I must dispose of one which I cannot accept. Whenever a person who already has enough to live on proposes to engage in some everyday kind of job, such as school-teaching or typing, he or she is told that such conduct takes the bread out of other people's mouths, and is therefore wicked. If this argument were valid, it would only be necessary for us all to be idle in order that we should all have our mouths full of bread. What people who say such things forget is that what a man earns he usually spends, and in spending he gives employment. As long as a man spends his income, he puts just as much bread into people's mouths in spending as he takes out of other people's mouths in earning. The real villain, from this point of view, is the man who saves. If he merely puts his savings in a stocking, like the proverbial French peasant, it is obvious that they do not give employment. If he invests his savings, the matter is less obvious, and different cases arise.

One of the commonest things to do with savings is to lend them to some Government. In view of the fact that the bulk of the public expenditure of most civilised Governments consists in payment for past wars or preparation for future wars, the man who lends his money to a Government is in the same position as the bad men in Shakespeare who hire murderers. The net result of the man's economical habits is to increase the armed forces of the State to which he lends his savings. Obviously it would be better if he spent the money, even if he spent it in drink or gambling.

But, I shall be told, the case is quite different when savings are invested in industrial enterprises. When such enterprises succeed, and produce something useful, this may be conceded. In these days, however, no one will deny that most enterprises fail. That means that a large amount of human labour, which might have been devoted to producing something that could be enjoyed, was expended on producing machines which, when produced, lay idle and did no good to anyone. The man who invests his savings in a concern that goes bankrupt is therefore injuring others as well as himself. If he spent his money, say, in giving parties for his friends, they (we may hope) would get pleasure, and so would all those upon whom he spent money, such as the butcher, the baker, and the bootlegger. But if he spends it (let us say) upon laying down rails for surface cars in some place where surface cars turn out to be not wanted, he has diverted a mass of labour into channels where it gives pleasure to no one. Nevertheless, when he becomes poor through the failure of his investment he will be regarded as a victim of undeserved misfortune, whereas the gay spendthrift, who has spent his money philanthropically, will be despised as a fool and a frivolous person.

All this is only preliminary. I want to say, in all seriousness, that a great deal of harm is being done in the modern world by belief in the virtuousness of WORK, and that the road to happiness and prosperity lies in an organised diminution of work.

First of all: what is work? Work is of two kinds: first, altering the position of matter at or near the earth's surface relatively to other such matter; second, telling other people to do so. The first kind is unpleasant and ill paid; the second is pleasant and highly paid. The second kind is capable of indefinite extension: there are not only those who give orders, but those who give advice as to what orders should be given. Usually two opposite kinds of advice are given simultaneously by two organised bodies of men; this is called politics. The skill required for this kind of work is not knowledge of the subjects as to which advice is given, but knowledge of the art of persuasive speaking and writing, i.e. of advertising.

Throughout Europe, though not in America, there is a third class of men, more respected than either of the classes of workers. There are men who, through ownership of land, are able to make others pay for the privilege of being allowed to exist and to work. These landowners are idle, and I might therefore be expected to praise them. Unfortunately, their idleness is only rendered possible by the industry of others; indeed their desire for comfortable idleness is historically the source of the whole gospel of work. The last thing they have ever wished is that others should follow their example.

From the beginning of civilisation until the Industrial Revolution, a man could, as a rule, produce by hard work little more than was required for the subsistence of himself and his family, although his wife worked at least as hard as he did, and his children added their labour as soon as they were old enough to do so. The small surplus above bare necessaries was not left to those who produced it, but was appropriated by warriors and priests. In times of famine there was no surplus; the warriors and priests, however, still secured as much as at other times, with the result that many of the workers died of hunger. This system persisted in Russia until 1917,[2] and still persists in the East; in England, in spite of the Industrial Revolution, it remained in full force throughout the Napoleonic wars, and until a hundred years ago, when the new class of manufacturers acquired power. In America, the system came to an end with the Revolution, except in the South, where it persisted until the Civil War. A system which lasted so long and ended so recently has naturally left a profound impress upon men's thoughts and opinions. Much that we take for granted about the desirability of work is derived from this system, and, being pre-industrial, is not adapted to the modern world. Modern technique has made it possible for leisure, within limits, to be not the prerogative of small privileged classes, but a right evenly distributed throughout

[2] Since then, members of the Communist Party have succeeded to this privilege of the warriors and priests.

the community. The morality of work is the morality of slaves, and the modern world has no need of slavery.

It is obvious that, in primitive communities, peasants, left to themselves, would not have parted with the slender surplus upon which the warriors and priests subsisted, but would have either produced less or consumed more. At first, sheer force compelled them to produce and part with the surplus. Gradually, however, it was found possible to induce many of them to accept an ethic according to which it was their duty to work hard, although part of their work went to support others in idleness. By this means the amount of compulsion required was lessened, and the expenses of government were diminished. To this day, 99 per cent of British wage-earners would be genuinely shocked if it were proposed that the King should not have a larger income than a working man. The conception of duty, speaking historically, has been a means used by the holders of power to induce others to live for the interests of their masters rather than for their own. Of course the holders of power conceal this fact from themselves by managing to believe that their interests are identical with the larger interests of humanity. Sometimes this is true; Athenian slave-owners, for instance, employed part of their leisure in making a permanent contribution to civilisation which would have been impossible under a just economic system. Leisure is essential to civilisation, and in former times leisure for the few was only rendered possible by the labours of the many. But their labours were valuable, not because work is good, but because leisure is good. And with modern technique it would be possible to distribute leisure justly without injury to civilisation.

Modern technique has made it possible to diminish enormously the amount of labour required to secure the necessaries of life for everyone. This was made obvious during the war. At that time all the men in the armed forces, all the men and women engaged in the production of munitions, all the men and women engaged in spying, war propaganda, or Government

offices connected with the war, were withdrawn from productive occupations. In spite of this, the general level of physical
well-being among unskilled wage-earners on the side of the
Allies was higher than before or since. The significance of this
fact was concealed by finance: borrowing made it appear as if the
future was nourishing the present. But that, of course, would
have been impossible; a man cannot eat a loaf of bread that does
not yet exist. The war showed conclusively that, by the scientific
organisation of production, it is possible to keep modern populations in fair comfort on a small part of the working capacity of
the modern world. If, at the end of the war, the scientific organisation, which had been created in order to liberate men for
fighting and munition work, had been preserved, and the hours
of work had been cut down to four, all would have been well.
Instead of that the old chaos was restored, those whose work was
demanded were made to work long hours, and the rest were left
to starve as unemployed. Why? because work is a duty, and a
man should not receive wages in proportion to what he has
produced, but in proportion to his virtue as exemplified by his
industry.

This is the morality of the Slave State, applied in circumstances
totally unlike those in which it arose. No wonder the result has
been disastrous. Let us take an illustration. Suppose that, at a
given moment, a certain number of people are engaged in the
manufacture of pins. They make as many pins as the world
needs, working (say) eight hours a day. Someone makes an
invention by which the same number of men can make twice as
many pins as before. But the world does not need twice as many
pins: pins are already so cheap that hardly any more will be
bought at a lower price. In a sensible world, everybody concerned in the manufacture of pins would take to working four
hours instead of eight, and everything else would go on as
before. But in the actual world this would be thought demoralising. The men still work eight hours, there are too many pins,

some employers go bankrupt, and half the men previously concerned in making pins are thrown out of work. There is, in the
end, just as much leisure as on the other plan, but half the men
are totally idle while half are still overworked. In this way, it is
insured that the unavoidable leisure shall cause misery all round
instead of being a universal source of happiness. Can anything
more insane be imagined?

The idea that the poor should have leisure has always been
shocking to the rich. In England, in the early nineteenth century,
fifteen hours was the ordinary day's work for a man; children
sometimes did as much, and very commonly did twelve hours a
day. When meddlesome busybodies suggested that perhaps
these hours were rather long, they were told that work kept
adults from drink and children from mischief. When I was a
child, shortly after urban working men had acquired the vote,
certain public holidays were established by law, to the great
indignation of the upper classes. I remember hearing an old
Duchess say: 'What do the poor want with holidays? They ought
to work.' People nowadays are less frank, but the sentiment persists, and is the source of much of our economic confusion.

Let us, for a moment, consider the ethics of work frankly,
without superstition. Every human being, of necessity, con-
sumes, in the course of his life, a certain amount of the produce
of human labour. Assuming, as we may, that labour is on the
whole disagreeable, it is unjust that a man should consume more
than he produces. Of course he may provide services rather
than commodities, like a medical man, for example; but he
should provide something in return for his board and lodging.
To this extent, the duty of work must be admitted, but to this
extent only.

I shall not dwell upon the fact that, in all modern societies
outside the USSR, many people escape even this minimum
amount of work, namely all those who inherit money and all
those who marry money. I do not think the fact that these people

are allowed to be idle is nearly so harmful as the fact that wage-earners are expected to overwork or starve.

If the ordinary wage-earner worked four hours a day, there would be enough for everybody, and no unemployment—assuming a certain very moderate amount of sensible organisation. This idea shocks the well-to-do, because they are convinced that the poor would not know how to use so much leisure. In America men often work long hours even when they are already well off; such men, naturally, are indignant at the idea of leisure for wage-earners, except as the grim punishment of unemployment; in fact, they dislike leisure even for their sons. Oddly enough, while they wish their sons to work so hard as to have no time to be civilised, they do not mind their wives and daughters having no work at all. The snobbish admiration of uselessness, which, in an aristocratic society, extends to both sexes, is, under a plutocracy, confined to women; this, however, does not make it any more in agreement with common sense.

The wise use of leisure, it must be conceded, is a product of civilisation and education. A man who has worked long hours all his life will be bored if he becomes suddenly idle. But without a considerable amount of leisure a man is cut off from many of the best things. There is no longer any reason why the bulk of the population should suffer this deprivation; only a foolish asceticism, usually vicarious, makes us continue to insist on work in excessive quantities now that the need no longer exists.

In the new creed which controls the government of Russia, while there is much that is very different from the traditional teaching of the West, there are some things that are quite unchanged. The attitude of the governing classes, and especially of those who conduct educational propaganda, on the subject of the dignity of labour, is almost exactly that which the governing classes of the world have always preached to what were called the 'honest poor'. Industry, sobriety, willingness to work long hours for distant advantages, even submissiveness to authority, all these reappear; moreover authority still represents the will of the Ruler of the Universe, Who, however, is now called by a new name, Dialectical Materialism.

The victory of the proletariat in Russia has some points in common with the victory of the feminists in some other countries. For ages, men had conceded the superior saintliness of women, and had consoled women for their inferiority by maintaining that saintliness is more desirable than power. At last the feminists decided that they would have both, since the pioneers among them believed all that the men had told them about the desirability of virtue, but not what they had told them about the worthlessness of political power. A similar thing has happened in Russia as regards manual work. For ages, the rich and their sycophants have written in praise of 'honest toil', have praised the simple life, have professed a religion which teaches that the poor are much more likely to go to heaven than the rich, and in general have tried to make manual workers believe that there is some special nobility about altering the position of matter in space, just as men tried to make women believe that they derived some special nobility from their sexual enslavement. In Russia, all this teaching about the excellence of manual work has been taken seriously, with the result that the manual worker is more honoured than anyone else. What are, in essence, revivalist appeals are made, but not for the old purposes: they are made to secure shock workers for special tasks. Manual work is the ideal which is held before the young, and is the basis of all ethical teaching.

For the present, possibly, this is all to the good. A large country, full of natural resources, awaits development, and has to be developed with very little use of credit. In these circumstances, hard work is necessary, and is likely to bring a great reward. But what will happen when the point has been reached where everybody could be comfortable without working long hours?

In the West, we have various ways of dealing with this problem. We have no attempt at economic justice, so that a large proportion of the total produce goes to a small minority of the population, many of whom do no work at all. Owing to the absence of any central control over production, we produce hosts of things that are not wanted. We keep a large percentage of the working population idle, because we can dispense with their labour by making the others overwork. When all these methods prove inadequate, we have a war: we cause a number of people to manufacture high explosives, and a number of others to explode them, as if we were children who had just discovered fireworks. By a combination of all these devices we manage, though with difficulty, to keep alive the notion that a great deal of severe manual work must be the lot of the average man.

In Russia, owing to more economic justice and central control over production, the problem will have to be differently solved. The rational solution would be, as soon as the necessaries and elementary comforts can be provided for all, to reduce the hours of labour gradually, allowing a popular vote to decide, at each stage, whether more leisure or more goods were to be preferred. But, having taught the supreme virtue of hard work, it is difficult to see how the authorities can aim at a paradise in which there will be much leisure and little work. It seems more likely that they will find continually fresh schemes, by which present leisure is to be sacrificed to future productivity. I read recently of an ingenious plan put forward by Russian engineers, for making the White Sea and the northern coasts of Siberia warm, by putting a dam across the Kara Sea. An admirable project, but liable to postpone proletarian comfort for a generation, while the nobility of toil is being displayed amid the ice-fields and snowstorms of the Arctic Ocean. This sort of thing, if it happens, will be the result of regarding the virtue of hard work as an end in itself, rather than as a means to a state of affairs in which it is no longer needed.

The fact is that moving matter about, while a certain amount of it is necessary to our existence, is emphatically not one of the ends of human life. If it were, we should have to consider every navvy superior to Shakespeare. We have been misled in this matter by two causes. One is the necessity of keeping the poor contented, which has led the rich, for thousands of years, to preach the dignity of labour, while taking care themselves to remain undignified in this respect. The other is the new pleasure in mechanism, which makes us delight in the astonishingly clever changes that we can produce on the earth's surface. Neither of these motives makes any great appeal to the actual worker. If you ask him what he thinks the best part of his life, he is not likely to say: 'I enjoy manual work because it makes me feel that I am fulfilling man's noblest task, and because I like to think how much man can transform his planet. It is true that my body demands periods of rest, which I have to fill in as best I may, but I am never so happy as when the morning comes and I can return to the toil from which my contentment springs.' I have never heard working men say this sort of thing. They consider work, as it should be considered, a necessary means to a livelihood, and it is from their leisure hours that they derive whatever happiness they may enjoy.

It will be said that, while a little leisure is pleasant, men would not know how to fill their days if they had only four hours of work out of the twenty-four. In so far as this is true in the modern world, it is a condemnation of our civilisation; it would not have been true at any earlier period. There was formerly a capacity for light-heartedness and play which has been to some extent inhibited by the cult of efficiency. The modern man thinks that everything ought to be done for the sake of something else, and never for its own sake. Serious-minded persons, for example, are continually condemning the habit of going to the cinema, and telling us that it leads the young into crime. But all the work that goes to producing a cinema is respectable, because it is work, and because it brings a money profit. The notion that the desirable activities are those that bring a profit has made everything topsy-turvy. The butcher who provides you with meat and the baker who provides you with bread are praiseworthy, because they are making money; but when you enjoy the food they have provided, you are merely frivolous, unless you eat only to get strength for your work. Broadly speaking, it is held that getting money is good and spending money is bad. Seeing that they are two sides of one transaction, this is absurd; one might as well maintain that keys are good, but keyholes are bad. Whatever merit there may be in the production of goods must be entirely derivative from the advantage to be obtained by consuming them. The individual, in our society, works for profit; but the social purpose of his work lies in the consumption of what he produces. It is this divorce between the individual and the social purpose of production that makes it so difficult for men to think clearly in a world in which profit-making is the incentive to industry. We think too much of production, and too little of consumption. One result is that we attach too little importance to enjoyment and simple happiness, and that we do not judge production by the pleasure that it gives to the consumer.

When I suggest that working hours should be reduced to four, I am not meaning to imply that all the remaining time should necessarily be spent in pure frivolity. I mean that four hours' work a day should entitle a man to the necessities and elementary comforts of life, and that the rest of his time should be his to use as he might see fit. It is an essential part of any such social system that education should be carried further than it usually is at present, and should aim, in part, at providing tastes which would enable a man to use leisure intelligently. I am not thinking mainly of the sort of things that would be considered 'highbrow'. Peasant dances have died out except in remote rural areas, but the impulses which caused them to be cultivated must still exist in human nature. The pleasures of urban populations have become mainly passive: seeing cinemas, watching football matches, listening to the radio, and so on. This results from the fact that their active energies are fully taken up with work; if they had more leisure, they would again enjoy pleasures in which they took an active part.

In the past, there was a small leisure class and a larger working class. The leisure class enjoyed advantages for which there was no basis in social justice; this necessarily made it oppressive, limited its sympathies, and caused it to invent theories by which to justify its privileges. These facts greatly diminished its excellence, but in spite of this drawback it contributed nearly the whole of what we call civilisation. It cultivated the arts and discovered the sciences; it wrote the books, invented the philosophies, and refined social relations. Even the liberation of the oppressed has usually been inaugurated from above. Without the leisure class, mankind would never have emerged from barbarism.

The method of a hereditary leisure class without duties was, however, extraordinarily wasteful. None of the members of the class had been taught to be industrious, and the class as a whole was not exceptionally intelligent. The class might produce one Darwin, but against him had to be set tens of thousands of country gentlemen who never thought of anything more intelligent than fox-hunting and punishing poachers. At present, the universities are supposed to provide, in a more systematic way, what the leisure class provided accidentally and as a by-product. This is a great improvement, but it has certain drawbacks. University life is so different from life in the world at large that men who live in an academic milieu tend to be unaware of the preoccupations and problems of ordinary men and women; moreover their ways of expressing themselves are usually such as to rob their opinions of the influence that they ought to have upon the general public. Another disadvantage is that in universities studies are organised, and the man who thinks of some original line of research is likely to be discouraged. Academic institutions, therefore, useful as they are, are not adequate guardians of the interests of civilisation in a world where everyone outside their walls is too busy for unutilitarian pursuits.

In a world where no one is compelled to work more than four hours a day, every person possessed of scientific curiosity will be able to indulge it, and every painter will be able to paint without starving, however excellent his pictures may be. Young writers will not be obliged to draw attention to themselves by sensational pot-boilers, with a view to acquiring the economic independence needed for monumental works, for which, when the time at last comes, they will have lost the taste and the capacity. Men who, in their professional work, have become interested in some phase of economics or government, will be able to develop their ideas without the academic detachment that makes the work of university economists often seem lacking in reality. Medical men will have time to learn about the progress of medicine, teachers will not be exasperatedly struggling to teach by routine methods things which they learnt in their youth, which may, in the interval, have been proved to be untrue.

Above all, there will be happiness and joy of life, instead of frayed nerves, weariness, and dyspepsia. The work exacted will be enough to make leisure delightful, but not enough to produce exhaustion. Since men will not be tired in their spare time, they will not demand only such amusements as are passive and vapid. At least one per cent will probably devote the time not spent in professional work to pursuits of some public importance, and, since they will not depend upon these pursuits for their livelihood, their originality will be unhampered, and there will be no need to conform to the standards set by elderly pundits. But it is not only in these exceptional cases that the advantages of leisure will appear. Ordinary men and women, having the opportunity of a happy life, will become more kindly and less persecuting and less inclined to view others with suspicion. The taste for war will die out, partly for this reason, and partly because it will involve long and severe work for all. Good nature is, of all moral qualities, the one that the world needs most, and good nature is the result of ease and security, not of a life of arduous struggle. Modern methods of production have given us the possibility of ease and security for all; we have chosen, instead, to have overwork for some and starvation for the others. Hitherto we have continued to be as energetic as we were before there were machines; in this we have been foolish, but there is no reason to go on being foolish for ever.

2

'USELESS' KNOWLEDGE

Francis Bacon, a man who rose to eminence by betraying his friends, asserted, no doubt as one of the ripe lessons of experience, that 'knowledge is power'. But this is not true of *all* knowledge. Sir Thomas Browne wished to know what song the sirens sang, but if he had ascertained this it would not have enabled him to rise from being a magistrate to being High Sheriff of his county. The sort of knowledge that Bacon had in mind was that which we call scientific. In emphasising the importance of science, he was belatedly carrying on the tradition of the Arabs and the early Middle Ages, according to which knowledge consisted mainly as astrology, alchemy, and pharmacology, all of which were branches of science. A learned man was one who, having mastered these studies, had acquired magical powers. In the early eleventh century, Pope Silvester II, for no reason except that he read books, was universally believed to be a magician in league with the devil. Prospero, who in Shakespeare's time was a mere phantasy, represented what had been for centuries the generally received conception of a learned man, so far at least as his powers of sorcery were concerned. Bacon believed—rightly, as we now know—that science could provide a more powerful magician's wand than any that had been dreamed of by the necromancers of former ages.

The renaissance, which was at its height in England at the time of Bacon, involved a revolt against the utilitarian conception of knowledge. The Greeks had acquired a familiarity with Homer, as we do with music hall songs, because they enjoyed him, and without feeling that they were engaged in the pursuit of learning. But the men of the sixteenth century could not begin to understand him without first absorbing a very considerable amount of linguistic erudition. They admired the Greeks, and did not wish to be shut out from their pleasures; they therefore copied them, both in reading the classics and in other less avowable ways. Learning, in the renaissance, was part of the *joie de vivre*, just as much as drinking or love-making. And this was true not only of literature, but also of sterner studies. Everyone knows the story of Hobbes's first contact with Euclid: opening the book, by chance, at the theorem of Pythagoras, he exclaimed, 'By God, this is impossible', and proceeded to read the proofs backwards until, reaching the axioms, he became convinced. No one can doubt that this was for him a voluptuous moment, unsullied by the thought of the utility of geometry in measuring fields.

It is true that the renaissance found a practical use for the ancient languages in connection with theology. One of the earliest results of the new feeling for classical Latin was the discrediting of the forged decretals and the donation of Constantine. The inaccuracies which were discovered in the Vulgate and the Septuagint made Greek and Hebrew a necessary part of the controversial equipment of Protestant divines. The republican maxims of Greece and Rome were invoked to justify the resistance of Puritans to the Stuarts and of Jesuits to monarchs who had thrown off allegiance to the Pope. But all this was an effect, rather than a cause, of the revival of classical learning, which had been in full swing in Italy for nearly a century before Luther. The main motive of the renaissance was mental delight, the restoration of a certain richness and freedom in art and speculation which had been lost while ignorance and superstition kept the mind's eye in blinkers.

The Greeks, it was found, had devoted a part of their attention to matters not purely literary or artistic, such as philosophy, geometry, and astronomy. These studies, therefore, were respectable, but other sciences were more open to question. Medicine, it was true, was dignified by the names of Hippocrates and Galen; but in the intervening period it had become almost confined to Arabs and Jews, and inextricably intertwined with magic. Hence the dubious reputation of such men as Paracelsus. Chemistry was in even worse odour, and hardly became respectable until the eighteenth century.

In this way it was brought about that knowledge of Greek and Latin, with a smattering of geometry and perhaps astronomy, came to be considered the intellectual equipment of a gentleman. The Greeks disdained the practical applications of geometry, and it was only in their decadence that they found a use for astronomy in the guise of astrology. The sixteenth and seventeenth centuries, in the main, studied mathematics with Hellenic disinterestedness, and tended to ignore the sciences which had been degraded by their connection with sorcery. A gradual change towards a wider and more practical conception of knowledge, which was going on throughout the eighteenth century, was suddenly accelerated at the end of that period by the French Revolution and the growth of machinery, of which the former gave a blow to gentlemanly culture while the latter offered new and astonishing scope for the exercise of ungentlemanly skill. Throughout the last hundred and fifty years, men have questioned more and more vigorously the value of 'useless' knowledge, and have come increasingly to believe that the only knowledge worth having is that which is applicable to some part of the economic life of the community.

In countries such as France and England, which have a traditional educational system, the utilitarian view of knowledge has only partially prevailed. There are still, for example, professors of Chinese in the universities who read the Chinese classics but are unacquainted with the works of Sun Yat-sen, which created modern China. There are still men who know ancient history in so far as it was related by authors whose style was pure, that is to say up to Alexander in Greece and Nero in Rome, but refuse to know the much more important later history because of the literary inferiority of the historians who related it. Even in France and England, however, the old tradition is dying, and in more up to date countries, such as Russia and the United States, it is utterly extinct. In America, for example, educational commissions point out that fifteen hundred words are all that most people employ in business correspondence, and therefore suggest that all others should be avoided in the school curriculum. Basic English, a British invention, goes still further, and reduces the necessary vocabulary to eight hundred words. The conception of speech as something capable of aesthetic value is dying out, and it is coming to be thought that the sole purpose of words is to convey practical information. In Russia the pursuit of practical aims is even more whole-hearted than in America: all that is taught in educational institutions is intended to serve some obvious purpose in education or government. The only escape is afforded by theology: the sacred scriptures must be studied by some in the original German, and a few professors must learn philosophy in order to defend dialectical materialism against the criticism of bourgeois metaphysicians. But as orthodoxy becomes more firmly established, even this tiny loophole will be closed.

Knowledge, everywhere, is coming to be regarded not as a good in itself, or as a means of creating a broad and humane outlook on life in general, but as merely an ingredient in technical skill. This is part of the greater integration of society which has been brought about by scientific technique and military necessity. There is more economic and political interdependence than there was in former times, and therefore there is more social pressure to compel a man to live in a way that his neighbours think useful. Educational establishments, except those for the very rich, or (in England) such as have become invulnerable through antiquity, are not allowed to spend their money as they like, but must satisfy the State that they are serving a useful purpose by imparting skill and instilling loyalty. This is part and parcel of the same movement which has led to compulsory military service, boy scouts, the organisation of political parties, and the dissemination of political passion by the Press. We are all more aware of our fellow-citizens than we used to be, more anxious, if we are virtuous, to do them good, and in any case to make them do us good. We do not like to think of anyone lazily enjoying life, however refined may be the quality of his enjoyment. We feel that everybody ought to be doing something to help on the great cause (whatever it may be), the more so as so many bad men are working against it and ought to be stopped. We have not leisure of mind, therefore, to acquire any knowledge except such as will help us in the fight for whatever it may happen to be that we think important.

There is much to be said for the narrowly utilitarian view of education. There is not time to learn everything before beginning to make a living, and undoubtedly 'useful' knowledge is very useful. It has made the modern world. Without it, we should not have machines or motor-cars or railways or aeroplanes; it should be added that we should not have modern advertising or modern propaganda. Modern knowledge has brought about an immense improvement in average health, and at the same time has discovered how to exterminate large cities by poison gas. Whatever is distinctive of our world, as compared with former times, has its source in 'useful' knowledge. No community as yet has enough of it, and undoubtedly education must continue to promote it.

It must also be admitted that a great deal of the traditional cultural education was foolish. Boys spent many years acquiring Latin and Greek grammar, without being, at the end, either capable or desirous (except in a small percentage of cases) of reading a Greek or Latin author. Modern languages and history are preferable, from every point of view, to Latin and Greek. They are not only more useful, but they give much more culture in much less time. For an Italian of the fifteenth century, since practically everything worth reading, if not in his own language, was in Greek or Latin, these languages were the indispensable keys to culture. But since that time great literatures have grown up in various modern languages, and the development of civilisation has been so rapid that knowledge of antiquity has become much less useful in understanding our problems than knowledge of modern nations and their comparatively recent history. The traditional schoolmaster's point of view, which was admirable at the time of the revival of learning, became gradually unduly narrow, since it ignored what the world has done since the fifteenth century. And not only history and modern languages, but science also, when properly taught, contributes to culture. It is therefore possible to maintain that education should have other aims than direct utility, without defending the traditional curriculum. Utility and culture, when both are conceived broadly, are found to be less incompatible than they appear to the fanatical advocates of either.

Apart, however, from the cases in which culture and direct utility can be combined, there is indirect utility, of various different kinds, in the possession of knowledge which does not contribute to technical efficiency. I think some of the worst features of the modern world could be improved by a greater encouragement of such knowledge and a less ruthless pursuit of mere professional competence.

When conscious activity is wholly concentrated on some one definite purpose, the ultimate result, for most people, is lack of balance accompanied by some form of nervous disorder. The men who directed German policy during the war made mistakes, for example, as regards the submarine campaign which brought America on to the side of the Allies, which any person coming fresh to the subject could have seen to be unwise, but which they could not judge sanely owing to mental concentration and lack of holidays. The same sort of thing may be seen wherever bodies of men attempt tasks which put a prolonged strain upon spontaneous impulses. Japanese imperialists, Russian Communists, and German Nazis all have a kind of tense fanaticism which comes of living too exclusively in the mental world of certain tasks to be accomplished. When the tasks are as important and as feasible as the fanatics suppose, the result may be magnificent; but in most cases narrowness of outlook has caused oblivion of some powerful counteracting force, or has made all such forces seem the work of the devil, to be met by punishment and terror. Men as well as children have need of play, that is to say, of periods of activity having no purpose beyond present enjoyment. But if play is to serve its purpose, it must be possible to find pleasure and interest in matters not connected with work.

The amusements of modern urban populations tend more and more to be passive and collective, and to consist of inactive observation of the skilled activities of others. Undoubtedly such amusements are much better than none, but they are not as good as would be those of a population which had, through education, a wider range of intelligent interests not connected with work. Better economic organisation, allowing mankind to benefit by the productivity of machines, should lead to a very great increase of leisure, and much leisure is apt to be tedious except to those who have considerable intelligent activities and interests. If a leisured population is to be happy, it must be an educated population, and must be educated with a view to mental enjoyment as well as to the direct usefulness of technical knowledge.

The cultural element in the acquisition of knowledge, when it is successfully assimilated, forms the character of a man's thoughts and desires, making them concern themselves, in part at least, with large impersonal objects, not only with matters of immediate importance to himself. It has been too readily assumed that, when a man has acquired certain capacities by means of knowledge, he will use them in ways that are socially beneficial. The narrowly utilitarian conception of education ignores the necessity of training a man's purposes as well as his skill. There is in untrained human nature a very considerable element of cruelty, which shows itself in many ways, great and small. Boys at school tend to be unkind to a new boy, or to one whose clothes are not quite conventional. Many women (and not a few men) inflict as much pain as they can by means of malicious gossip. The Spaniards enjoy bull-fights; the British enjoy hunting and shooting. The same cruel impulses take more serious forms in the hunting of Jews in Germany and kulaks in Russia. All imperialism affords scope for them, and in war they become sanctified as the highest form of public duty.

Now it must be admitted that highly educated people are sometimes cruel, I think there can be no doubt that they are less often so than people whose minds have lain fallow. The bully in a school is seldom a boy whose proficiency in learning is up to the average. When a lynching takes place, the ring-leaders are almost invariably very ignorant men. This is not because mental cultivation produces positive humanitarian feelings, though it may do so; it is rather because it gives other interests than the ill-treatment of neighbours, and other sources of self-respect than the assertion of domination. The two things most universally desired are power and admiration. Ignorant men can, as a rule, only achieve either by brutal means, involving the acquisition of physical mastery. Culture gives a man less harmful forms of power and more deserving ways of making himself admired. Galileo did more than any monarch has done to change the world, and his power immeasurably exceeded that of his persecutors. He had therefore no need to aim at becoming a persecutor in his turn.

Perhaps the most important advantage of 'useless' knowledge is that it promotes a contemplative habit of mind. There is in the world too much readiness, not only for action without adequate previous reflection, but also for some sort of action on occasions on which wisdom would counsel inaction. People show their bias on this matter in various curious ways. Mephistopheles tells the young student that theory is grey but the tree of life is green, and everyone quotes this as if it were Goethe's opinion, instead of what he supposes the devil would be likely to say to an undergraduate. Hamlet is held up as an awful warning against thought without action, but no one holds up Othello as a warning against action without thought. Professors such as Bergson, from a kind of snobbery towards the practical man, decry philosophy, and say that life at its best should resemble a cavalry charge. For my part, I think action is best when it emerges from a profound apprehension of the universe and human destiny, not from some wildly passionate impulse of romantic but disproportioned self-assertion. A habit of finding pleasure in thought rather than in action is a safeguard against unwisdom and excessive love of power, a means of preserving serenity in misfortune and peace of mind among worries. A life confined to what is personal is likely, sooner or later, to become unbearably painful; it is only by windows into a larger and less fretful cosmos that the more tragic parts of life become endurable.

A contemplative habit of mind has advantages ranging from the most trivial to the most profound. To begin with minor vexations, such as fleas, missing trains, or cantankerous business associates. Such troubles seem hardly worthy to be met by reflections on the excellence of heroism or the transitoriness of all human ills, and yet the irritation to which they give rise destroys many people's good temper and enjoyment of life. On such occasions, there is much consolation to be found in out of the way bits of knowledge which have some real or fancied connection with the trouble of the moment; or even if they have none, they serve to obliterate the present from one's thoughts. When assailed by people who are white with fury, it is pleasant to remember the chapter in Descartes' *Treatise on the Passions* entitled 'Why those who grow pale with rage are more to be feared than those who grow red.' When one feels impatient over the difficulty of securing international co-operation, one's impatience is diminished if one happens to think of the sainted King Louis IX, before embarking on his crusade, allying himself with the Old Man of the Mountain, who appears in the Arabian Nights as the dark source of half the wickedness in the world. When the rapacity of capitalists grows oppressive, one may be suddenly consoled by the recollection that Brutus, that exemplar of republican virtue, lent money to a city at 40 per cent, and hired a private army to besiege it when it failed to pay the interest.

Curious learning not only makes unpleasant things less unpleasant, but also makes pleasant things more pleasant. I have enjoyed peaches and apricots more since I have known that they were first cultivated in China in the early days of the Han dynasty; that Chinese hostages held by the great King Kaniska introduced them into India, whence they spread to Persia, reaching the Roman Empire in the first century of our era; that the word 'apricot' is derived from the same Latin source as the word 'precocious', because the apricot ripens early; and that the A at the beginning was added by mistake, owing to a false etymology. All this makes the fruit taste much sweeter.

About a hundred years ago, a number of well-meaning philanthropists started societies 'for the diffusion of useful knowledge', with the result that people have ceased to appreciate the delicious savour of 'useless' knowledge. Opening Burton's *Anatomy of Melancholy* at haphazard on a day when I was threatened by that mood, I learnt that there is a 'melancholy matter', but that, while some think it may be engendered of all four humours, 'Galen holds that it may be engendered of three alone, excluding phlegm or pituita, whose true assertion Valerius and Menardus stiffly maintain, and so doth Fuscius, Montaltus, Montanus. How (say they) can white become black?' In spite of this unanswerable argument, Hercules de Saxonia and Cardan, Guianerius and Laurentius, are (so Burton tells us) of the opposite opinion. Soothed by these historical reflections, my melancholy, whether due to three humours or to four, was dissipated. As a cure for too much zeal, I can imagine a few measures more effective than a course of such ancient controversies.

But while the trivial pleasures of culture have their place as a relief from the trivial worries of practical life, the more important merits of contemplation are in relation to the greater evils of life, death and pain and cruelty, and the blind march of nations into unnecessary disaster. For those to whom dogmatic religion can no longer bring comfort, there is need of some substitute, if life is not to become dusty and harsh and filled with trivial self-assertion. The world at present is full of angry self-centred groups, each incapable of viewing human life as a whole, each willing to destroy civilisation rather than yield an inch. To this narrowness no amount of technical instruction will provide an antidote. The antidote, in so far as it is a matter of individual psychology, is to be found in history, biology, astronomy, and all those studies which, without destroying self-respect, enable the individual to see himself in his proper perspective. What is needed is not this or that specific piece of information, but such knowledge as inspires a conception of the ends of human life as a whole: art and history, acquaintance with the lives of heroic individuals, and some understanding of the strangely accidental and ephemeral position of man in the cosmos—all this touched with an emotion of pride in what is distinctively human, the power to see and to know, to feel magnanimously and to think with understanding. It is from large perceptions combined with impersonal emotion that wisdom most readily springs.

Life, at all times full of pain, is more painful in our time than in the two centuries that preceded it. The attempt to escape from pain drives men to triviality, to self-deception, to the invention of vast collective myths. But these momentary alleviations do but increase the sources of suffering in the long run. Both private and public misfortune can only be mastered by a process in which will and intelligence interact: the part of will is to refuse to shirk the evil or accept an unreal solution, while the part of intelligence is to understand it, to find a cure if it is curable, and, if not, to make it bearable by seeing it in its relations, accepting it as unavoidable, and remembering what lies outside it in other regions, other ages, and the abysses of interstellar space.

3

ARCHITECTURE AND SOCIAL QUESTIONS

Architecture, from the earliest times, has had two purposes: on the one hand, the purely utilitarian one of affording warmth and shelter; on the other, the political one of impressing an idea upon mankind by means of the splendour of its expression in stone. The former purpose sufficed as regards the dwellings of the poor; but the temples of gods and the palaces of kings were designed to inspire awe for the heavenly powers and for their earthly favourites. In a few cases, it was not individual monarchs but communities that were glorified: the Acropolis at Athens and the Capitol in Rome showed forth the imperial majesty of those proud cities for the edification of subjects and allies. Aesthetic merit was considered desirable in public buildings, and, later on, in the palaces of plutocrats and emperors, but was not aimed at in the hovels of peasants or the rickety tenements of the urban proletariat.

In the mediaeval world, in spite of a greater complexity in the social structure, the artistic motive in architecture was similarly restricted, indeed even more so, for the castles of the great were designed for military strength, and if they had beauty it was by accident. It was not feudalism, but the Church and commerce that gave rise to the best building in the Middle Ages. The cathedrals displayed the glory of God and His bishops. The wool trade between England and the Low Countries, which knew the Kings of England and the Dukes of Burgundy to be its hirelings, embodied its pride in the splendid cloth halls and municipal buildings of Flanders, and, less magnificently, in many English market places. But it was Italy, the birthplace of modern plutocracy, that brought commercial architecture to perfection. Venice, the bride of the sea, the city that diverted crusades and overawed the united monarchs of Christendom, created a new type of stately beauty in the Doge's palace and in those of the merchant princes. Unlike the rustic barons of the North, the urban magnates of Venice and Genoa had no need of solitude and defence, but lived side by side, and created cities in which everything visible to the not-too-inquisitive stranger was splendid and aesthetically satisfying. In Venice, especially, the concealment of squalor was easy: the slums were hidden away in back alleys, and were never seen by the users of gondolas. Never since has plutocracy achieved so complete and perfect a success.

The Church, in the Middle Ages, built not only cathedrals, but also buildings of another sort, more relevant to our modern needs: abbeys, monasteries, nunneries, and colleges. These were based upon a restricted form of Communism, and designed for peaceful social life. In these buildings, everything individual was Spartan and simple, everything communal, was splendid and spacious. The humility of the single monk was satisfied with a hard bare cell; the pride of the order was displayed in the large magnificence of halls and chapels and refectories. In England, monasteries and abbeys survive mainly as ruins to please tourists, but colleges, at Oxford and Cambridge, are still part of the national life, and retain the beauty of mediaeval communalism.

With the spread of the renaissance into the North, the uncouth barons of France and England set to work to acquire the polish of the Italian rich. While the Medici married their daughters to kings, poets, painters, and architects north of the Alps copied Florentine models, and aristocrats replaced their castles by country houses, which, by their defencelessness against assault, marked the new security of a courtly and civilised nobility. But the security was destroyed by the French Revolution, and since that time the traditional styles of architecture have lost their vitality. They linger where the older forms of power linger, as in Napoleon's additions to the Louvre; but these additions have a florid vulgarity which shows his insecurity. He seems to be trying to forget his mother's constant remark in bad French: 'Pourvou que cela doure.'

There are two typical forms of architecture in the nineteenth century, due respectively to machine production and democratic individualism: on the one hand the factory with its chimneys, on the other the rows of tiny houses for working-class families. While the factory represents the economic organisation brought about by industrialism, the little houses represent the social separateness which is the ideal of an individualistic population. Where high ground rents make large buildings desirable, they have a merely architectural, not a social, unity: they are blocks of offices, apartment houses, or hotels, whose occupants do not form a community like the monks in a monastery, but endeavour, as far as possible, to remain unaware of each other's existence. Wherever, in England, the value of the land is not too great, the principle of one house for each family reasserts itself. As one approaches London or any large northern town by rail, one passes endless streets of such small dwellings, where each house is a centre of individual life, the communal life being represented by the office, the factory, or the mine, according to the locality. Social life outside the family, so far as architecture can secure such a result, is exclusively economic, and all non-economic social needs must be satisfied within the family or remain thwarted. If the social ideals of an age are to be judged by the aesthetic quality of its architecture, the last hundred years represent the lowest point yet reached by humanity.

The factory and the rows of small houses, between them, illustrate a curious inconsistency in modern life. While production has become increasingly a matter in which large groups are concerned, our general outlook, in everything that we regard as outside the sphere of politics and economics, has tended to become more and more individualistic. This is true not only in matters of art and culture, where the cult of self-expression has led to an anarchic revolt against every kind of tradition and convention, but also—perhaps as a reaction against overcrowding—in the daily lives of ordinary men, and still more of ordinary women. In the factory, perforce, there is social life, which has produced the trade unions; but at home each family desires isolation. 'I keep myself to myself,' women say; and their husbands like to think of them sitting at home waiting for the return of the master of the house. These feelings make wives endure, and even prefer, the separate little house, the separate little kitchen, the separate drudgery at housework, and the separate care of children while they are not at school. The work is hard, the life monotonous, and the woman almost a prisoner in her own house; yet all this, though it frays her nerves, she prefers to a more communal way of life, because separateness ministers to her self-respect.

The preference for this type of architecture is connected with the status of women. In spite of feminism and the vote, the position of wives, at any rate in the wage-earning class, is not much changed from what it was. The wife still depends upon her husband's earnings, and does not receive wages although she works hard. Being professionally a housekeeper, she likes to have a house to keep. The desire to have scope for personal initiative, which is common to most human beings, has for her no outlet except in the home. The husband, on his side, enjoys the feeling that his wife works for him and is economically dependent upon him; moreover his wife and his house provide more satisfaction for his instinct of property than would be possible with any different type of architecture. From conjugal possessiveness, both husband and wife, if at any time they feel a wish for a more social life, are nevertheless each glad that the other has so few occasions to meet possibly dangerous members of the opposite sex. And so, though their lives may be cramped and the woman's unnecessarily laborious, neither desires a different organisation of their social existence.

All this would be changed if it were the rule, and not the exception, for married women to earn their living by work outside the home. In the professional class there are already enough wives earning money by independent work to produce, in big towns, some approach to what their circumstances make desirable. What such women need is a service flat or a communal kitchen to relieve them of the care of meals, and a nursery school to take charge of the children during office hours. Conventionally, a married woman is supposed to regret the necessity of working away from home, and if, at the end of her day, she has to do the jobs ordinarily done by wives who have no other occupation, she is likely to be seriously over-worked. But given the right type of architecture, women could be relieved of most of the work of housekeeping and minding children, with advantage to themselves, their husbands, and their children, and in that case the substitution of professional work for the traditional duties of wives and mothers would be a clear gain. Every husband of an old-fashioned wife would be convinced of this, if, for a week, he were to attempt over his wife's duties.

The work of a wage-earner's wife has never been modernised because it is unpaid, but in fact much of it is unnecessary, and the rest should, for the most part, be divided among different specialists. But if this is to be done, the first reform required is an architectural reform. The problem is to secure the same communal advantages as were secured in mediaeval monasteries, but without celibacy; that is to say, there must be provision for the needs of children.

Let us first consider what are the unnecessary disadvantages of the present system in which each working-class household is self-contained, whether in the form of a separate house or of rooms in a block of tenements.

The gravest evils fall upon the children. Before they are of school age, they have far too little sun and air; their diet is that provided by a mother who is poor, ignorant, and busy, and unable to provide one sort of meal for adults and another for the young; they are constantly getting in the way while their mother cooks and does her work, with the result that they get on her nerves and receive harsh treatment, perhaps alternating with caresses; they never have liberty or space or an environment in which their natural activities are innocuous. This combination of circumstances tends to make them rickety, neurotic, and subdued.

The evils for the mother are also very serious. She has to combine the duties of nurse, cook, and housemaid, for none of which she has been trained; almost inevitably she performs them all badly; she is always tired, and finds her children a bother instead of a source of happiness; her husband is at leisure when his work stops, but she never has leisure; in the end, almost inevitably, she becomes irritable, narrow-minded, and full of envy.

For the man the disadvantages are less, since he is less in the home. But when he is at home he is not likely to enjoy his wife's querulousness or the 'bad' behaviour of the children; because he blames his wife when he ought to blame the architecture, with unpleasant consequences which vary with the degree of his brutality.

I do not say, of course, that all this happens universally, but I do say that, when it does not, there has to be an exceptional amount of self-discipline, wisdom, and physical vigour in the mother. And obviously a system which demands exceptional qualities of human beings will only be successful in exceptional cases. The badness of such a system is not disproved by the existence of rare instances in which its evils do not appear.

To cure all these troubles simultaneously, it is only necessary to introduce a communal element into architecture. The separate little houses, and the blocks of tenements each with its own kitchen, should be pulled down. In their place there should be high blocks of buildings round a central quadrangle, the south side being left low to admit the sunshine. There should be a common kitchen, a spacious dining hall, and another hall for amusements and meetings and the cinema. In the central quad-rangle there should be a nursery school, constructed in such a way that the children could not easily do harm either to them-selves or to fragile objects: there should be no steps, no open fires or hot stoves exposed to the touch, plates and cups and saucers should be made of unbreakable material, and generally there should be the utmost possible avoidance of those things that make it necessary to say 'don't' to children. In good weather, the nursery school should be in the open air; in bad weather, except the very worst, in rooms open to the air at one side. All the children's meals should be in the nursery school, which could, quite cheaply, provide them with a more wholesome diet than their mothers can give them. From the time they are weaned until they go to school, they should spend all the time from breakfast till after their last meal at the nursery school, where they should have opportunities of amusing themselves, but the very minimum of supervision compatible with their safety.

The gain to the children would be enormous. Their health would benefit by air and sun and space and good food; their character would benefit by freedom and by escape from the atmosphere of constant querulous prohibition in which most wage-earners spend their first years. Liberty of movement, which can only be safely allowed to a young child in a specially constructed environment, could be almost unchecked in the nursery school, with the result that adventurousness and muscular skill would develop naturally as they do in young animals. The constant prohibition of movement in young children is a source of discontent and timidity in later life, but is largely unavoidable so long as they live in an adult environment; the nursery school, therefore, would be as beneficial to their character as to their health.

For women the advantages would be quite as great. As soon as their children were weaned, they would hand them over, throughout the day, to women specially trained in the care of young children. They would not have the business of buying food, cooking it, and washing up. They would go out to work in the mornings and come home in the evenings, like their husbands; like their husbands, they would have hours of work and hours of leisure, instead of being always busy. They would see their children in the morning and evening, long enough for affection, but not long enough for frayed nerves. Mothers who are with their children all day long hardly ever have enough superfluous energy to play with them; as a rule, fathers play with their children much more than mothers do. Even the most affectionate adult is bound to find children trying if there is never a moment's rest from their clamorous demands for attention. But at the end of a day spent apart, both mother and children would feel more affectionate than is possible when they are cooped up together all day. The children, physically tired but mentally at peace, would enjoy their mother's attentions after the impartiality of the women at the nursery school. What is good in family life would survive, without what is worrying and destructive of affection.

For men and women equally there would be an escape from the confinement of small rooms and sordidness into large public rooms, which might be as architecturally splendid as College Halls. Beauty and space need no longer be the prerogative of the rich. There would be an end to the irritation that comes of being cooped up at close quarters, and that too often makes family life impossible.

And all this would be the consequence of an architectural reform.

Robert Owen, more than a hundred years ago, incurred much ridicule for his 'co-operative parallelograms', which were an attempt to secure for wage earners the advantages of collegiate life. Although the suggestion was premature in those days of grinding poverty, many parts of it have now come much nearer to what is practicable and desirable. He himself, at New Lanark, was able to establish a nursery school on very enlightened principles. But he was misled by the special circumstances of New Lanark into regarding his 'parallelograms' as productive units, not merely as places of residence. The tendency of industrialism has been, from the first, to lay too much stress on production, and too little on consumption and ordinary living; this has been a result of emphasis on profits, which are associated only with production. The result is that the factory has become scientific, and has carried division of labour to the farthest possible point, while the home has remained unscientific, and still heaps the most diverse labours upon the head of the overburdened mother. It is a natural result of the domination of the profit-making motive that the most haphazard, unorganised, and altogether unsatisfactory departments of human activity are those from which no pecuniary profit is to be expected.

It must be admitted, however, that the most powerful obstacles to such architectural reform as I have been suggesting are to be found in the psychology of the wage-earners themselves. However they may quarrel, people like the privacy of the 'home', and find in it a satisfaction to pride and possessiveness. A celibate communal life, such as that of monasteries, did not raise the same problem; it is marriage and the family that introduce the instinct of privacy. I do not think private cooking, beyond what could be done occasionally on a gas-ring, is really necessary to satisfy this instinct; I believe that a private apartment with one's own furniture would suffice for people who were used to it. But it is always difficult to change intimate habits. The desire of women for independence, however, may lead gradually more and more to women earning their living outside the home, and this, in turn, may make such a system as we have been considering seem to them desirable. At present, feminism is still at an early stage of development among women of the wage-earning class, but it is likely to increase unless there is a Fascist reaction. Perhaps in time this motive may lead women to prefer communal cooking and the nursery school. It will not be from men that a desire for the change will come. Wage-earning men, even when they are Socialists or Communists, seldom see any need for an alteration in the status of their wives.

While unemployment remains a grave evil, and while failure to understand economic principles remains almost universal, the employment of married women is naturally objected to as likely to throw out of work those whose jobs the married women secure. For this reason, the problem of married women are bound up with the problem of unemployment, which is probably insoluble without a very considerable degree of Socialism. In any case, however, the construction of 'co-operative parallelograms' such as I have been advocating could only come, on a large scale, as part of a large Socialistic movement, since the profit motive alone could never bring it about. The health and character of children, and the nerves of wives, must therefore continue to suffer so long as the desire for profit regulates economic activities. Some things can be achieved by this motive, and some cannot; among those that cannot is the well-being of wives and children in the wage-earning class, and—what may seem even more Utopian—giving beauty to suburbs. But although we take the hideousness of suburbs for granted, like March winds and November fogs, it has not, in fact, the same inevitability. If they were constructed by municipal instead of private enterprise, with planned streets, and houses like the Courts of Colleges, there is no reason why they should not be a delight to the eye. Hideousness, as much as worry and poverty, is part of the price we pay for our slavery to the motive of private profit.

4

THE MODERN MIDAS[1]

The story of King Midas and the Golden Touch is familiar to all who were brought up on Hawthorne's *Tanglewood Tales*. This worthy king, being abnormally fond of gold, was granted by a god the privilege that everything he touched turned to gold. At first he was delighted, but when he found that the food he wished to eat became solid metal before he could swallow it, he began to feel worried; and when his daughter became petrified as he kissed her, he was aghast, and begged the god to take his gift away again. From this moment he realised that gold is not the only thing of value.

This is a simple story, but its moral is one that the world finds very hard to learn. When the Spaniards, in the sixteenth century, acquired the gold of Peru, they thought it desirable to retain it in their own hands, and they put all sorts of obstacles in the way of the export of the precious metals. The consequence was that the gold merely raised prices throughout the Spanish dominions,

[1] Written in 1932.

without making Spain any richer than before in actual goods. It might be a satisfaction to a man's pride to feel that he had twice as much money as before, but if each doubloon only purchased half what it used to purchase, the gain was purely metaphysical, and did not enable him to have more food and drink or a better house or any other tangible advantage. The English and Dutch, being less powerful than the Spaniards, were obliged to content themselves with what is now the Eastern United States, a region that was despised because it contained no gold. But as a source of wealth this region has proved immeasurably more productive than the gold-producing parts of the New World which all nations coveted in the time of Elizabeth.

Although, as a matter of history, this has become a common-place, its application to present-day problems seems to be beyond the mental capacity of Governments. The subject of economics has always been viewed in a topsy-turvy way, and this is more true now than at any previous time. What happened at the end of the war, in this respect, is so absurd that it is difficult to believe that the Governments were composed of grown-up men not in lunatic asylums. They wanted to punish Germany, and the time-honoured way of doing this was to impose an indemnity. So they imposed an indemnity. So far, so good. But the amount that they wished Germany to pay was enormously greater than all the gold in Germany, or even in the world. It was therefore mathematically impossible for the Germans to pay except in goods; the Germans had to pay in goods or not at all.

At this point the Governments suddenly remembered that they had the habit of measuring a nation's prosperity by the excess of exports over imports. When a country exports more than it imports, it is said to have a favourable balance of trade; in the contrary case, the balance is said to be unfavourable. But by imposing upon Germany an indemnity greater than could be paid in gold, they had decreed that in trade with the Allies Germany was to have a favourable balance of trade and the Allies were to have an unfavourable balance. To their horror, they found that they had unintentionally been doing Germany what they considered a benefit by stimulating her export trade. To this general argument, others more specific were added. Germany produces nothing that cannot be produced by the Allies, and the threat of German competition was everywhere resented. The English did not want German coal when their own coal-mining industry was depressed. The French did not want German iron and steel manufactures when they were engaged in increasing their own iron and steel production by the help of the newly acquired Lorraine ore. And so on. The Allies, therefore, while remaining determined to punish Germany by making her pay, were equally determined not to let her make the payment in any particular form.

To this lunatic situation a lunatic solution was found. It was decided to lend Germany whatever Germany had to pay. The Allies said in effect: 'We cannot let you off the indemnity, because it is a just punishment for your wickedness; on the other hand, we cannot let you pay it, because that would ruin our industries; so we will lend you the money and you shall pay us back what we lend. In that way, the principle will be safeguarded without harm to ourselves. As for the harm to you, we hope that that is only postponed.'

But this solution, obviously could only be temporary. The subscribers to German loans wanted their interest, and there was the same dilemma about paying the interest as there had been about paying the indemnity. The Germans could not pay the interest in gold, and the Allied nations did not wish them to pay in goods. So it became necessary to lend them the money to pay the interest. It is obvious that, sooner or later, people were bound to get tired of this game. When people are tired of lending to a country without getting any return, the country's credit is said to be no longer good. When this happens, people begin to demand the actual payment of what is due to them. But, as we have seen, this was impossible for the Germans. Hence many bankruptcies, first in Germany, then among those to whom bankrupt Germans owed money, then among those to whom those people owed money, and so on. Result, universal depression, misery, starvation, ruin, and the whole train of disasters from which the world has been suffering.

I do not mean to suggest that German indemnities were the sole cause of our troubles. The debts of the Allies to America contributed, and so, in a lesser degree, did all debts, private and public, where debtor and creditor were separated by a high tariff wall, so that payment in goods was difficult. The German indemnity, while by no means the whole source of the trouble, is, however, one of the clearest instances of the confusion of thought which has made the trouble so difficult to deal with.

The confusion of thought from which our misfortunes have arisen is the confusion between the standpoint of the consumer and that of the producer, or, more correctly, of the producer under a competitive system. When the indemnities were imposed, the Allies regarded themselves as consumers: they considered that it would be pleasant to have the Germans work for them as temporary slaves, and to be able themselves to consume, without labour, what the Germans had produced. Then, after the Treaty of Versailles had been concluded, they suddenly remembered that they were also producers, and that the influx of German goods which they had been demanding would ruin their industries. They were so puzzled that they started scratching their heads, but that did no good, even when they all did it together and called it an International Conference. The plain fact is that the governing classes of the world are too ignorant and stupid to be able to think through such a problem, and too conceited to ask advice of those who might help them.

To simplify our problem, let us suppose that one of the Allied nations consisted of a single individual, a Robinson Crusoe living on a desert island. The Germans would be obliged, under the

Treaty of Versailles, to offer him all the necessaries of life for nothing. But if he behaved as the Powers have behaved, he would say: 'No, do not bring me coal, because it will ruin my wood-gathering industry; do not bring me bread, because it will ruin my agriculture and my ingenious though primitive milling apparatus; do not bring me clothes, because I have an infant industry of making clothes out of the skins of beasts. I do not mind if you bring me gold, because that can do me no harm; I will put it in a cave, and make no use of it whatever. But on no account will I accept payment in any form that I could make use of.' If our imaginary Robinson Crusoe said this, we should think that solitude had deprived him of his wits. Yet that is exactly what all the leading nations have said to Germany. When a nation, instead of an individual, is seized with lunacy, it is thought to be displaying remarkable industrial wisdom.

The only relevant difference between Robinson Crusoe and a whole nation is that Robinson Crusoe organises his time sensibly and a nation does not. If an individual gets his clothes for nothing, he does not spend his time making clothes. But nations think that they ought to produce everything that they need, except where there is some natural obstacle such as climate. If nations had sense, they would arrange, by international agreement, which nation was to produce what, and would no more attempt to produce everything than individuals do. No individual tries to make his own clothes, his own shoes, his own food, his own house, and so on; he knows quite well that, if he did, he would have to be content with a very low level of comfort. But nations do not yet understand the principle of division of labour. If they did, they could have let Germany pay in certain classes of goods, which they would have ceased to make themselves. The men who would have been thrown out of work could have been taught another trade at the public expense. But this would have required organisation of production, which is contrary to business orthodoxy.

Superstitions about gold are curiously deep-seated, not only in those who profit by them, but even in those to whom they bring misfortune. In the autumn of 1931, when the French forced the English to abandon the gold standard, they imagined that they were doing the English an injury, and the English, for the most part, agreed with them. A sort of shame, a feeling as of national humiliation, swept over England. Yet all the best economists had been urging abandonment of the gold standard, and subsequent experience has proved that they were right. So ignorant are the men in practical control of banking that the British Government had to be compelled by force to do what was best for British interests, and that only French unfriendliness led France to confer this unintended benefit upon England.

Of all reputedly useful occupations, about the most absurd is gold-mining. Gold is dug out of the earth in South Africa, and is conveyed, with infinite precautions against theft and accident, to London or Paris or New York, where it is again placed underground in the vaults of banks. It might just as well have been left underground in South Africa. There was, possibly, some utility in bank reserves so long as it was held that on occasion they might be used, but as soon as the policy was adopted of never letting them sink below a certain minimum, that amount was rendered as good as non-existent. If I say I will put by £100 against a rainy day, I may be wise. But if I say that, however poor I may become, I will not spend the £100, it ceases to be an effective part of my fortune, and I might just as well have given it away. This is exactly the situation as regards bank reserves if they are not to be spent in any circumstances whatever. It is, of course, merely a relic of barbarism that any part of national credit should still be based upon actual gold. In private transactions within a country, the use of gold has died out. Before the war it was still used for small sums, but people who have grown up since the war hardly know the look of a gold coin. Nevertheless it is still supposed that, by some mysterious hocus-pocus, everybody's financial stability depends upon a hoard of gold in the central bank of his country. During the war, when submarines made it dangerous to transport gold, the fiction was carried still further. Of the gold that was mined in South Africa, some was deemed to be in the United States, some in England, some in France, and so on, but in fact it all stayed in South Africa. Why not carry the fiction a stage farther, and deem that the gold has been mined, while leaving it quietly in the ground?

The advantage of gold, in theory, is that it affords a safeguard against the dishonesty of Governments. This would be all very well if there were any way of forcing Governments to adhere to gold in a crisis, but in fact they abandon gold whenever it suits them to do so. All the European countries that took part in the late war depreciated their currencies, and in so doing repudiated a part of their debts. Germany and Austria repudiated the whole of their internal debt by inflation. France reduced the franc to a fifth of its former value, thereby repudiating four-fifths of all Government debts that were reckoned in francs. The pound sterling is worth only about three-quarters of its former value in gold. The Russians frankly said that they would not pay their debts, but this was thought wicked: respectable repudiation demands a certain etiquette.

The fact is that Governments, like other people, pay their debts if it is to their interest to do so, but not otherwise. A purely legal guarantee, such as the gold standard, is useless in times of stress, and unnecessary at other times. A private individual finds it profitable to be honest so long as he is likely to wish to borrow again and to be able to do so, but when he has exhausted his credit he may find it more advantageous to abscond. A Government is in a different position towards its own subjects from that in which it finds itself towards other countries. Its own subjects are at its mercy, and it therefore has no motive for honesty towards them except desire to borrow again. When, as happened in Germany after the war, there is no longer any prospect of internal borrowing, it pays a country to let its currency become worthless, and thus wipe out the whole internal debt. But external debt is another matter. The Russians, when they repudiated their debts to other countries, had to face war against the whole civilised world, combined with a ferocious hostile propaganda. Most nations are not in a position to face this sort of thing, and are therefore cautious as regards external debt. It is this, not the gold standard, that affords what security exists in lending money to Governments. The security is poor, but cannot be made better until there is an international Government.

The extent to which economic transactions depend upon armed forces is not usually realised. Ownership of wealth is acquired, in part, by means of skill in business, but such skill is only possible within a framework of military or naval prowess. It was by the use of armed force that New York was taken by the Dutch from the Indians, by the English from the Dutch, and by the Americans from the English. When oil was found in the United States, it belonged to American citizens; but when oil is found in some less powerful country, the ownership of it comes, by hook or by crook, to the citizens of some one or other of the Great Powers. The process by which this is effected is usually disguised, but in the background lurks the threat of war, and it is this latent threat which clinches negotiations.

What applies to oil applies equally to currency and debt. When it is to the interest of a Government to debase its currency or repudiate its debts, it does so. Some nations, it is true, make a great fuss about the moral importance of paying one's debts, but they are creditor nations. In so far as they are listened to by debtor nations, it is because of their strength, not because they are ethically convincing. There is therefore only one way of securing a stable currency, and that is to have, in fact if not in form, a single world Government, possessed of the sole effective armed forces. Such a Government would have an interest in a stable currency, and could decree a currency with a constant purchasing power in terms of the average of commodities. This is the only true stability, and gold does not possess it. Nor will sovereign nations adhere even to gold in times of stress. The argument that gold secures a stable currency is therefore from every point of view fallacious.

I have been informed repeatedly, by persons who considered themselves hard-headed realists, that men in business normally desire to grow rich. Observation has convinced me that the persons who gave me this assurance, so far from being realists, were sentimental idealists, totally blind to the most patent facts of the world in which they live. If business men really wished to grow rich more ardently than they wish to keep others poor, the world would quickly become a paradise. Banking and currency afford an admirable example. It is obviously to the general interest of the business community as a whole to have a stable currency and security of credit. To secure these two desiderata, it is obviously necessary to have only one central bank in the world, and only one currency, which must be a paper currency so managed as to keep average prices as nearly constant as possible. Such a currency will not need to be based upon a gold reserve, but upon the credit of the world Government of which the one central bank is the financial organ. All this is so obvious that any child can see it. Yet nothing of the sort is advocated by business men. Why? Because of nationalism, that is to say, because they are more anxious to keep foreigners poor than to grow rich themselves.

Another reason is the psychology of the producer. It seems like a truism that money is only useful because it can be exchanged for goods, and yet there are few people to whom this is true emotionally as well as rationally. In almost every transaction, the seller is more pleased than the buyer. If you buy a pair of shoes, the whole apparatus of salesmanship is brought to bear upon you, and the seller of the shoes feels as if he had won a little victory. You, on the other hand, do not say to yourself:

'How nice to have got rid of those nasty dirty bits of paper, which I could neither eat nor use as clothing, and to have got instead a lovely new pair of shoes.' We regard our buying as unimportant in comparison with our selling. The only exceptions are cases in which the supply is limited. A man who buys an Old Master is more pleased than the man who sells it; but when the Old Master was alive, he was no doubt more pleased to sell pictures than his patrons were to buy them. The ultimate psychological source of our preference for selling over buying is that we prefer power to pleasure. This is not a universal characteristic: there are spendthrifts, who like a short life and a merry one. But it is a characteristic of the energetic, successful individuals who give the tone to a competitive age. When most wealth was inherited, the psychology of the producer was less dominant than it is now. It is the psychology of the producer that makes men more anxious to sell than to buy, and that causes Governments to engage in the laughable attempt to create a world in which every nation sells and no nation buys.

The psychology of the producer is complicated by a circumstance which distinguishes economic relations from most others. If you produce and sell some commodity, there are two classes of mankind who are specially important to you, namely, your competitors and your customers. Your competitors harm you, and your customers benefit you. Your competitors are obvious and comparatively few, whereas your customers are diffused and for the most part unknown. You tend, therefore, to be more conscious of your competitors than of your customers. This may not be the case within your own group, but it is almost sure to be the case where an alien group is concerned, so that alien groups come to be regarded as having economic interests adverse to our own. The belief in protective tariffs is derived from this source. Foreign nations are regarded rather as competitors in production than as possible customers, so that men are willing to lose foreign markets to avoid foreign competition.

There was once a butcher in a small town who was infuriated by the other butchers who took away his custom. In order to ruin them, he converted the whole town to vegetarianism, and was surprised to find that as a result he was ruined too. The folly of this man seems incredible, yet it is no greater than that of all the Powers. All have observed that foreign trade enriches other nations, and all have erected tariffs to destroy foreign trade. All have been astonished to find that they were as much injured as their competitors. Not one has remembered that trade is reciprocal, and that a foreign nation which sells to one's own nation also buys from it either directly or indirectly. The reason that they have not remembered that is that hatred of foreign nations has made them incapable of clear thinking where foreign trade is concerned.

In Great Britain, the conflict between rich and poor, which has been the basis of party divisions ever since the end of the war, has made most industrialists incapable of understanding questions of currency. Since finance represents wealth, there is a tendency for all the rich to follow the lead of the bankers and financiers. But in fact the interests of bankers have been opposed to the interests of industrialists: deflation suited the bankers, but paralysed British industry. I do not doubt that, if wage-earners had not had votes, British politics since the war would have consisted of a bitter struggle between financiers and industrialists. As things were, however, financiers and industrialists combined against wage-earners, the industrialists supported the financiers, and the country was brought to the verge of ruin. It was saved only by the fact that the financiers were defeated by the French.

Throughout the world, not only in Great Britain, the interests of finance in recent years have been opposed to the interests of the general public. This state of affairs is not likely to change of itself. A modern community is not likely to be prosperous if its financial affairs are conducted solely with a view to the interests of financiers, and without regard to the effect upon the rest of the population. When this is the case, it is unwise to leave financiers to the unfettered pursuit of their private profit. One might as well run a museum for the profit of the curator, leaving him at liberty to sell the contents whenever he happened to be offered a good price. There are some activities in which the motive of private profit leads, on the whole, to the promotion of the general interest, and others in which this is not so. Finance is now definitely in the latter class, whatever it may have been in the past. The result is an increasing need of governmental interference with finance. It will be necessary to consider finance and industry as forming a single whole, and to aim at maximising the profits of the whole, not of the financial part separately. Finance is more powerful than industry when both are independent, but the interests of industry more nearly coincide with those of the community than do the interests of finance. This is the reason that the world has been brought to such a pass by the excessive power of finance.

Wherever the few have acquired power over the many, they have been assisted by some superstition which dominated the many. Ancient Egyptian priests discovered how to predict eclipses, which were still viewed with terror by the populace; in this way they were able to extort gifts and powers which they could not otherwise have obtained. Kings were supposed to be divine beings, and Cromwell was thought guilty of sacrilege when he cut off Charles I's head. In our day, financiers depend upon the superstitious reverence for gold. The ordinary citizen is struck dumb with awe when he is told about gold reserves, note issues, inflation, deflation, reflation, and all the rest of the jargon. He feels that anyone who can converse glibly about such matters must be very wise, and he does not dare to question what he is told. He does not realise what a small part gold really plays in modern transactions, though he would be quite at a loss to explain what its functions are. He feels vaguely that his country is likely to be safer if it contains a great deal of gold, so that he is glad when the gold reserve increases and sorry when it diminishes.

This condition of unintelligent respect on the part of the general public is exactly what the financier needs in order to remain unfettered by the democracy. He has, of course, many other advantages in dealing with opinion. Being immensely rich, he can endow universities, and secure that the most influential part of academic opinion shall be subservient to him. Being at the head of the plutocracy, he is the natural leader of all those whose political thought is dominated by fear of Communism. Being the possessor of economic power, he can distribute prosperity or ruin to whole nations as he chooses. But I doubt whether any of these weapons would suffice without the aid of superstition. It is a remarkable fact that, in spite of the importance of economics to every man, woman and child, the subject is almost never taught in schools and even in universities is learnt by a minority. Moreover, that minority do not learn the subject as it would be learnt if no political interests were at stake. There are a few institutions which teach it without plutocratic bias, but they are very few; as a rule, the subject is so taught as to glorify the economic *status quo*. All this, I fancy, is connected with the fact that superstition and mystery are useful to the holders of financial power.

Finance, like war, suffers from the fact that almost all those who have technical competence also have a bias which is contrary to the interests of the community. When Disarmament Conferences take place, the naval and military experts are the chief obstacle to their success. It is not that these men are dishonest, but that their habitual preoccupations prevent them from seeing questions concerning armaments in their proper perspective. Exactly the same thing applies to finance. Hardly anybody knows about it in detail except those who are engaged in making money out of the present system, who naturally cannot take wholly impartial views. It will be necessary, if this state of affairs is to be remedied, to make the democracies of the world aware of the importance of finance, and to find ways of simplifying the principles of finance so that they can be widely understood. It must be admitted that this is not easy, but I do not believe that it is impossible. One of the impediments to successful democracy in our age is the complexity of the modern world, which makes it increasingly difficult for ordinary men and women to form an intelligent opinion on political questions, or even to decide whose expert judgment deserves the most respect. The cure for this trouble is to improve education, and to find ways of explaining the structure of society which are easier to understand than those at present in vogue. Every believer in effective democracy must be in favour of this reform. But perhaps there are no believers in democracy left except in Siam and the remoter parts of Mongolia.

5

THE ANCESTRY OF FASCISM

When we compare our age with that of (say) George I, we are conscious of a profound change of intellectual temper, which has been followed by a corresponding change in the tone of politics. In a certain sense, the outlook of two hundred years ago may be called 'rational', and that which is most characteristic of our time may be called 'anti-rational'. But I want to use these words without implying a complete acceptance of the one temper or a complete rejection of the other. Moreover, it is important to remember that political events very frequently take their colour from the speculations of an earlier time: there is usually a considerable interval between the promulgation of a theory and its practical efficacy. English politics in 1860 were dominated by the ideas expressed by Adam Smith in 1776; German politics today are a realisation of theories set forth by Fichte in 1807; Russian politics since 1917 have embodied the doctrines of the Communist Manifesto, which dates from 1848. To understand the present age, therefore, it is necessary to go back to a considerably earlier time.

A widespread political doctrine has, as a rule, two very different kinds of causes. On the one hand, there are intellectual antecedents: men who have advanced theories which have grown, by development or reaction, from previous theories. On the other hand, there are economic and political circumstances which predispose people to accept views that minister to certain moods. These alone do not give a complete explanation when, as too often happens, intellectual antecedents are neglected. In the particular case that concerns us, various sections of the post-war world have had certain grounds of discontent which have made them sympathetic to a certain general philosophy invented at a much earlier date. I propose first to consider this philosophy, and then to touch on the reasons for its present popularity.

The revolt against *reason* began as a revolt against *reasoning*. In the first half of the eighteenth century, while Newton ruled men's minds, there was a widespread belief that the road to knowledge consisted in the discovery of simple general laws, from which conclusions could be drawn by deductive ratiocination. Many people forgot that Newton's law of gravitation was based upon a century of careful observation, and imagined that general laws could be discovered by the light of nature. There was natural religion, natural law, natural morality, and so on. These subjects were supposed to consist of demonstrative inferences from self-evident axioms, after the style of Euclid. The political outcome of this point of view was the doctrine of the Rights of Man, as preached during the American and French Revolutions.

But at the very moment when the Temple of Reason seemed to be nearing completion, a mine was laid by which, in the end, the whole edifice was blown sky-high. The man who laid the mine was David Hume. His *Treatise of Human Nature*, published in 1739, has as its sub-title 'An attempt to introduce the experimental method of reasoning into moral subjects'. This represents the whole of his intention, but only half of his performance. His intention was to substitute observation and induction for deduction from nominally self-evident axioms. In his temper of mind be was a complete rationalist, though of the Baconian rather than the Aristotelian variety. But his almost unexampled combination of acuteness with intellectual honesty led him to certain devastating conclusions: that induction is a habit without logical justification, and that the belief in causation is little better than a superstition. It followed that science, along with theology, should be relegated to the limbo of delusive hopes and irrational convictions.

In Hume, rationalism and scepticism existed peacefully side by side. Scepticism was for the study only, and was to be forgotten in the business of practical life. Moreover, practical life was to be governed, as far as possible, by those very methods of science which his scepticism impugned. Such a compromise was only possible for a man who was in equal parts a philosopher and a man of the world; there is also a flavour of aristocratic Toryism in the reservation of an esoteric unbelief for the initiated. The world at large refused to accept Hume's doctrines in their entirety. His followers rejected his scepticism, while his German opponents emphasised it as the inevitable outcome of a merely scientific and rational outlook. Thus as the result of his teaching British philosophy became superficial, while German philosophy became anti-rational—in each case from fear of an unbearable agnosticism. European thought has never recovered its previous wholeheartedness; among all the successors of Hume, sanity has meant superficiality, and profundity has meant some degree of madness. In the most recent discussions of the philosophy appropriate to quantum physics, the old debates raised by Hume are still proceeding.

The philosophy which has been distinctive of Germany begins with Kant, and begins as a reaction against Hume. Kant was determined to believe in causality, God, immortality, the moral law, and so on, but perceived that Hume's philosophy made all this difficult. He therefore invented a distinction between 'pure' reason and 'practical' reason. 'Pure' reason was concerned with what could be proved, which was not much; 'practical' reason was concerned with what was necessary for virtue, which was a great deal. It is of course obvious that 'pure' reason was simply reason, while 'practical' reason was prejudice. Thus Kant brought back into philosophy the appeal to something recognised as outside the sphere of theoretical rationality, which had been banished from the schools ever since the rise of scholasticism.

More important even than Kant, from our point of view, was his immediate successor Fichte, who, passing over from philosophy to politics, inaugurated the movement which has developed into National Socialism. But before speaking of him there is more to be said about the conception of 'reason'.

In view of the failure to find an answer to Hume, 'reason' can no longer be regarded as something absolute, any departure from which is to be condemned on theoretical grounds. Nevertheless, there is obviously a difference, and an important one, between the frame of mind of (say) the philosophical radicals and such people as the early Mohammedan fanatics. If we call the former temper of mind reasonable and the latter unreasonable, it is clear that there has been a growth of unreason in recent times.

I think that what we mean in practice by reason can be defined by three characteristics. In the first place, it relies upon persuasion rather than force; in the second place, it seeks to pursuade by means of arguments which the man who uses them believes to be completely valid; and in the third place, in forming opinions, it uses observation and induction as much as possible and intuition as little as possible. The first of these rules out the Inquisition; the second rules out such methods as those of British war propaganda, which Hitler praises on the ground that propaganda 'must sink its mental elevation deeper in proportion to the numbers of the mass whom it has to grip'; the third forbids the use of such a major premise as that of President Andrew Jackson apropos of the Mississippi, 'the God of the Universe intended this great valley to belong to one nation,' which was self-evident to him and his hearers, but not easily demonstrated to one who questioned it.

Reliance upon reason, as thus defined, assumes a certain community of interest and outlook between oneself and one's audience. It is true that Mrs Bond tried it on her ducks, when she cried, 'come and be killed, for you must be stuffed and my customers filled'; but in general the appeal to reason is thought ineffective with those whom we mean to devour. Those who believe in eating meat do not attempt to find arguments which would seem valid to a sheep, and Nietzsche does not attempt to persuade the mass of the population, whom he calls 'the bungled and botched'. Nor does Marx try to enlist the support of capitalists. As these instances show, the appeal to reason is easier when power is unquestioningly confined to an oligarchy. In eighteenth-century England, only the opinions of aristocrats and their friends were important, and these could always be presented in a rational form to other aristocrats. As the political constituency grows larger and more heterogeneous, the appeal to reason becomes more difficult, since there are fewer universally conceded assumptions from which agreement can start. When such assumptions cannot be found, men are driven to rely upon their own intuitions; and since the intuitions of different groups differ, reliance upon them leads to strife and power politics.

Revolts against reason, in this sense, are a recurrent phenomenon in history. Early Buddhism was reasonable; its later forms, and the Hinduism which replaced it in India, were not. In ancient Greece, the Orphics were in revolt against Homeric rationality. From Socrates to Marcus Aurelius, the prominent men in the ancient world were, in the main, rational; after Marcus Aurelius, even the conservative Neo-Platonists were filled with superstition. Except in the Mohammedan world, the claims of reason remained in abeyance until the eleventh century; after that, through scholasticism, the renaissance, and science, they became increasingly dominant. A reaction set in with Rousseau and Wesley, but was held in check by the triumphs of science and machinery in the nineteenth century. The belief in reason reached its maximum in the 'sixties; since then, it has gradually diminished, and is still diminishing. Rationalism and anti-rationalism have existed side by side since the beginning of Greek civilisation, and each, when it has seemed likely to become completely dominant, has always led, by reaction, to a new outburst of its opposite.

The modern revolt against reason differs in an important respect from most of its predecessors. From the Orphics onwards, the usual aim in the past was salvation—a complex concept involving both goodness and happiness, and achieved, as a rule, by some difficult renunciation. The irrationalists of our time aim, not at salvation, but at power. They thus develop an ethic which is opposed to that of Christianity and of Buddhism; and through their lust of dominion they are of necessity involved in politics. Their genealogy among writers is Fichte, Carlyle, Mazzini, Nietzsche—with supporters such as Treitschke, Rudyard Kipling, Houston Chamberlain, and Bergson. As opposed to this movement, Benthamites and Socialists may be viewed as two wings of one party: both are cosmopolitan, both are democratic, both appeal to economic self-interest. Their differences *inter se* are as to means, not ends, whereas the new movement, which culminates (as yet) in Hitler, differs from both as to ends, and differs even from the whole tradition of Christian civilisation.

The end which statesmen should pursue, as conceived by almost all the irrationalists out of whom Fascism has grown, is most clearly stated by Nietzsche. In conscious opposition to Christianity as well as to the utilitarians, he rejects Bentham's doctrine as regards both happiness and the 'greatest number'. 'Mankind', he says, 'is much more of means than an end . . . mankind is merely the experimental material.' The end he proposes is the greatness of exceptional individuals: 'The object is to attain that enormous *energy of greatness* which can model the man of the future by means of discipline and also by means of the annihilation of millions of the bungled and botched, and which can yet avoid *going to ruin* at the sight of the suffering *created thereby*, the like of which has never been seen before.' This conception of the end, it should be observed, cannot be regarded as in itself contrary to reason, since questions of ends are not amenable to rational argument. We may *dislike* it—I do myself—but we cannot *disprove* it any more than Nietzsche can prove it. There is, none the less, a natural connection with irrationality, since reason demands impartiality, whereas the cult of the great man always has as its minor premise the assertion: 'I am a great man.'

The founders of the school of thought out of which Fascism has grown all have certain common characteristics. They seek the good in will rather than in feeling or cognition; they value power more than happiness; they prefer force to argument, war to peace, aristocracy to democracy, propaganda to scientific impartiality. They advocate a Spartan form of austerity, as opposed to the Christian form; that is to say, they view austerity as a means of obtaining mastery over others, not as a self-discipline which helps to produce virtue, and happiness only in the next world. The later ones among them are imbued with popular Darwinism, and regard the struggle for existence as the source of a higher species; but it is to be rather a struggle between races than one between individuals, such as the apostles of free competition advocated. Pleasure and knowledge, conceived as ends, appear to them unduly passive. For pleasure they substitute glory, and, for knowledge, the pragmatic assertion that what they desire is true. In Fichte, Carlyle, and Mazzini, these doctrines are still enveloped in a mantle of conventional moralistic cant; in Nietzsche they first step forth naked and unashamed.

Fichte has received less than his due share of credit for inaugurating this great movement. He began as an abstract metaphysician, but showed even then a certain arbitrary and self-centred disposition. His whole philosophy develops out of the proposition 'I am I', as to which he says:

'The Ego *posits itself* and it is in consequence of this bare positing by itself; it is both the agent and the result of the action, the active and that which is produced by the activity; *I am* expresses a deed (*Thathandlung*). The Ego is, because it has posited itself.'

The Ego, according to this theory, exists because it wills to exist. Presently it appears that the non-Ego also exists because the Ego so wills it; but a non-Ego so generated never becomes really external to the Ego which chooses to posit it. Louis XIV said, 'l'état, c'est moi'; Fichte said, 'The universe is myself.' As Heine remarked in comparing Kant and Robespierre, 'in comparison with us Germans, you French are tame and moderate'.

Fichte, it is true, explains, after a while, that when he says 'I' he means 'God'; but the reader is now wholly reassured.

When, as a result of the Battle of Jena, Fichte had to fly from Berlin, he began to think that he had been too vigorously positing the non-Ego in the shape of Napoleon. On his return in 1807, he delivered his famous 'Addresses to the German Nation', in which, for the first time, the complete creed of nationalism was set out. These Addresses begin by explaining that the German is superior to all other moderns, because he alone has a pure language. (The Russians, Turks, and Chinese, not to mention the Eskimos and the Hottentots, also have pure languages, but they were not mentioned in Fichte's history books.) The purity of the German language makes the German alone capable of profundity; he concludes that 'to have character and to be German undoubtedly mean the same'. But if the German character is to be preserved from foreign corrupting influences, and if the German nation is to be capable of acting as a whole, there must be a new kind of education, which will 'mould the Germans into a corporate body'. The new education, he says, 'must consist essentially in this, that it completely destroys the freedom of the will'. He adds that will 'is the very root of man'.

There is to be no external commerce, beyond what is absolutely unavoidable. There is to be universal military service: everybody is to be compelled to fight, not for material well-being, not for freedom, not in defence of the constitution, but under the impulsion of 'the devouring flame of higher patriotism, which embraces the nation as the vesture of the eternal, for which the noble-minded man joyfully sacrifices himself, and the ignoble man, who only exists for the sake of the other, must likewise sacrifice himself.'

This doctrine, that the 'noble' man is the purpose of humanity, and that the 'ignoble' man has no claims on his own account, is of the essence of the modern attack on democracy. Christianity taught that every human being has an immortal soul, and that, in this respect, all men are equal; the 'rights of man' was only a development of Christian doctrine. Utilitarianism, while it conceded no absolute 'rights' to the individual, gave the same weight to one man's happiness as to another's; thus it led to democracy just as much as did the doctrine of natural rights. But Fichte, like a sort of political Calvin, picked out certain men as the elect, and rejected all the rest as of no account.

The difficulty, of course, is to know who are the elect. In a world in which Fichte's doctrine was universally accepted, every man would think that he was 'noble', and would join some party of people sufficiently similar to himself to seem to share some of his nobility. These people might be his nation, as in Fichte's case, or his class, as in that of a proletarian communist, or his family, as with Napoleon. There is no objective criterion of 'nobility' except success in war; therefore war is the necessary outcome of this creed.

Carlyle's outlook on life was, in the main, derived from Fichte, who was the strongest single influence on his opinions. But Carlyle added something which has been characteristic of the school ever since; a kind of Socialism and solicitude for the proletariat which is really dislike of industrialism and of the *nouveau riche*. Carlyle did this so well that he deceived even Engels, whose book on the English working class in 1844 mentions him with the highest praise. In view of this, we can scarcely wonder that many people were taken in by the socialistic façade in National Socialism.

Carlyle, in fact, still has his dupes. His 'hero worship' sounds very exalted; we need, he says, not elected Parliaments, but 'Hero-kings, and a whole world not unheroic'. To understand this, one must study its translation into fact. Carlyle, in *Past and Present*, holds up the twelfth-century Abbot Samson as a model; but whoever does not take that worthy on trust, but reads the *Chronicle of Jocelin of Brakelonde*, will find that the Abbot was an unscrupulous ruffian, combining the vices of a tyrannous land-lord with those of a pettifogging attorney. Carlyle's other heroes are at least equally objectionable. Cromwell's massacres in Ire-land move him to the comment: 'But in Oliver's time, as I say, there was still belief in the Judgments of God; in Oliver's time, there was yet no distracted jargon of "abolishing Capital Pun-ishments", of Jean-Jacques Philanthropy, and universal rose-water in this world still so full of sin. . . . Only in late decadent generations . . . can such indiscriminate mashing-up of Good and Evil into one universal patent-treacle . . . take effect in our earth'. Of most of his other heroes, such as Frederick the Great, Dr Francia, and Governor Eyre, all that need be said is that their one common characteristic was a thirst for blood.

Those who still think that Carlyle was in some sense more or less Liberal should read his chapter on Democracy in *Past and*

Present. Most of it is occupied with praise of William the Conqueror, and with a description of the pleasant lives enjoyed by serfs in his day. Then comes a definition of liberty: 'The true liberty of a man, you would say, consisted in his finding out, or being forced to find out the right path, and to walk thereon' (p. 263). He passes on to the statement that democracy 'means despair of finding any Heroes to govern you, and contented putting up with the want of them'. The chapter ends by stating, in eloquent prophetical language, that, when democracy shall have run its full course, the problem that will remain is 'that of finding government by your Real-Superiors'. Is there one word in all this to which Hitler would not subscribe?

Mazzini was a milder man than Carlyle, from whom he disagreed as regards the cult of heroes. Not the individual great man, but the nation, was the object of his adoration; and, while he placed Italy highest, he allowed a role to every European nation except the Irish. He believed, however, like Carlyle, that duty should be placed above happiness, above even collective happiness. He thought that God revealed to each human conscience what was right, and that all that was necessary was that everybody should obey the moral law as felt in his own heart. He never realised that different people may genuinely differ as to what the moral law enjoins, or that what he was really demanding was that others should act according to his revelation. He put morals above democracy, saying: 'The simple vote of a majority does not constitute sovereignty, if it evidently contradicts the supreme moral precepts . . . the will of the people is sacred, when it interprets and applies the moral law; null and impotent, when it dissociates itself from the law, and only represents caprice.' This is also the opinion of Mussolini.

Only one important element has since been added to the doctrines of this school, namely the pseudo-Darwinian belief in 'race'. (Fichte made German superiority a matter of language, not of biological heredity.) Nietzsche, who, unlike his followers, is not a nationalist or an anti-Semite, applies the doctrine only as between different individuals: he wishes the unfit to be prevented from breeding, and he hopes, by the methods of the dog-fancier, to produce a race of super-men, who shall have all power, and for whose benefit alone the rest of mankind shall exist. But subsequent writers with a similar outlook have tried to prove that all excellence has been connected with their own race. Irish professors write books to prove that Homer was an Irishman; French anthropologists give archaeological evidence that the Celts, not the Teutons, were the source of civilisation in Northern Europe; Houston Chamberlain argues at length that Dante was a German and Christ was not a Jew. Emphasis upon race has been universal among Anglo-Indians, from whom imperialist England caught the infection through the medium of Rudyard Kipling. But the anti-Semitic element has never been prominent in England, although an Englishman, Houston Chamberlain, was mainly responsible for giving it a sham historical basis in Germany, where it had persisted ever since the Middle Ages.

About race, if politics were not involved it would be enough to say that nothing politically important is known. It may be taken as probable that there are genetic mental differences between races; but it is certain that we do not yet know what these differences are. In an adult man, the effects of environment mask those of heredity. Moreover, the racial differences among different Europeans are less definite than those between white, yellow, and black men; there are no well-marked physical characteristics by which members of different modern European nations can be certainly known apart, since all have resulted from a mixture of different stocks. When it comes to mental superiority, every civilised nation can make out a plausible claim, which proves that all the claims are equally invalid. It is *possible* that the Jews are inferior to the Germans, but it is just as possible that the Germans are inferior to the Jews. The whole business of introducing pseudo-Darwinian jargon in such a question is utterly unscientific. Whatever we may come to know hereafter, we have not at present any good ground for wishing to encourage one race at the expense of another.

The whole movement, from Fichte onwards, is a method of bolstering up self-esteem and lust for power by means of beliefs which have nothing in their favour except that they are flattering. Fichte needed a doctrine which would make him feel superior to Napoleon; Carlyle and Nietzsche had infirmities for which they sought compensation in the world of imagination; British imperialism of Rudyard Kipling's epoch was due to shame at having lost industrial supremacy; and the Hitlerite madness of our time is a mantle of myth in which the German ego keeps itself warm against the cold blasts of Versailles. No man thinks sanely when his self-esteem has suffered a mortal wound, and those who deliberately humiliate a nation have only themselves to thank if it becomes a nation of lunatics.

This brings me to the reasons which have produced the wide acceptance of the irrational and even anti-rational doctrine that we have been considering. There are at most times all sorts of doctrines being preached by all sorts of prophets, but those which become popular must make some special appeal to the moods produced by the circumstances of the time. Now the characteristic doctrines of modern irrationalists, as we have seen, are: emphasis on will as opposed to thought and feeling; glorification of power; belief in intuitional 'positing' of prepositions as opposed to observational and inductive testing. This state of mind is the natural reaction of those who have the habit of controlling modern mechanisms such as aeroplanes, and also of those who have less power than formerly, but are unable to find any rational ground for the restoration of their former preponderance. Industrialism and the war, while giving the habit of mechanical power, caused a great shift of economic and political power, and therefore left large groups in the mood for pragmatic self-assertion. Hence the growth of Fascism.

Comparing the world of 1920 with that of 1820, we find that there had been an increase of power on the part of: large industrialists, wage-earners, women, heretics, and Jews. (By 'heretics' I mean those whose religion was not that of the Government of their country.) Correlatively, there had been a loss of power on the part of: monarchs, aristocracies, ecclesiastics, the lower middle classes, and males as opposed to females. The large industrialists, though stronger than at any previous period, felt themselves insecure owing to the threat of Socialism, and more particularly from fear of Moscow. The war interests—generals, admirals, aviators, and armament firms—were in the like case: strong at the moment, but menaced by a pestilential crew of Bolsheviks and pacifists. The sections already defeated—the kings and nobles, the small shopkeepers, the men who from temperament were opponents of religious toleration, and the men who regretted the days of masculine domination over women—seemed to be definitely down and out; economic and cultural developments, it was thought, had left no place for them in the modern world. Naturally they were discontented, and collectively they were numerous. The Nietzschean philosophy was psychologically adapted to their mental needs, and, very cleverly, the industrialists and militarists made use of it to weld the defeated sections into a party which should support a medievalist reaction in everything except industry and war. In regard to industry and war, there was to be everything modern in the way of technique, but not the sharing out of power and the effort after peace that made the Socialists dangerous to the existing magnates.

Thus the irrational elements in the Nazi philosophy are due, politically speaking, to the need of enlisting the support of sections which have no longer any *raison d'être*, while the comparatively sane elements are due to the industrialists and militarists. The former elements are 'irrational' because it is scarcely possible that the small shopkeepers, for example, should realise their hopes, and fantastic beliefs are their only refuge from despair; *per contra*, the hopes of industrialists and militarists might be realised by means of Fascism, but hardly in any other way. The fact that their hopes can only be achieved through the ruin of civilisation does not make them irrational, but only Satanic. These men form intellectually the best, and morally the worst, element in the movement; the rest, dazzled by the vision of glory, heroism, and self-sacrifice, have become blind to their serious interests, and in a blaze of emotion have allowed themselves to be used for purposes not their own. This is the psychopathology of Nazidom.

I have spoken of the industrialists and militarists who support Fascism as sane, but their sanity is only comparative. Thyssen believes that, by means of the Nazi movement, he can both kill Socialism and immensely increase his market. There seems, however, no more reason to think him right than there was to think that his predecessors were right in 1914. It is necessary for him to stir up German selfconfidence and nationalist feeling to a dangerous degree, and unsuccessful war is the most probable outcome. Even great initial successes would not bring ultimate victory; now, as twenty years ago, the German Government forgets America.

There is one very important element which is on the whole against the Nazis although it might have been expected to support reaction—I mean, organised religion. The philosophy of the movement which culminates in the Nazis is, in a sense, a logical development of Protestantism. The morality of Fichte and Carlyle is Calvinistic, and Mazzini, who was in lifelong opposition to Rome, had a thoroughly Lutheran belief in the infallibility of the individual conscience. Nietzsche believed passionately in the worth of the individual, and considered that the hero should not submit to authority; in this he was developing the Protestant spirit of revolt. It might have been expected that the

Protestant Churches would welcome the Nazi movement, and to a certain extent they did so. But in all these elements which Protestantism shared with Catholicism, it found itself opposed by the new philosophy. Nietzsche is emphatically anti-Christian, and Houston Chamberlain gives an impression that Christianity was a degraded superstition which grew up among the mongrel cosmopolitans of the Levant. The rejection of humility, of love of one's neighbour, and of the rights of the meek, is contrary to Gospel teaching; and anti-Semitism, when it is theoretical as well as practical, is not easily reconciled, with a religion of Jewish origin. For these reasons, Nazidom and Christianity have difficulty in making friends, and it is not impossible that their antagonism may bring about the downfall of the Nazis.

There is another reason why the modern cult of unreason, whether in Germany or elsewhere, is incompatible with any traditional form of Christianity. Inspired by Judaism, Christianity adopted the notion of Truth, with the correlative virtue of Faith. The notion and the virtue survived in 'honest doubt', as all the Christian virtues remained among Victorian free-thinkers. But gradually the influence of scepticism and advertising made it seem hopeless to discover truth, but very profitable to assert falsehood. Intellectual probity was thus destroyed. Hitler, explaining the Nazi programme, says:

'The national State will look upon science as a means for increasing national pride. Not only world history, but also the history of civilisation, must be taught from this point of view. The inventor should appear great, not merely as an inventor, but even more so as a fello-countryman. Admiration of any great deed must be combined with pride because the fortunate doer of it is a member of our own nation. We must extract the greatest from the mass of great names in German history and place them before the youth in so impressive a fashion that they may become the pillars of an unshakable nationalist sentiment.'

The conception of science as a pursuit of truth has so entirely disappeared from Hitler's mind that he does not even argue against it. As we know, the theory of relativity has come to be thought bad because it was invented by a Jew. The Inquisition rejected Galileo's doctrine because is considered it untrue; but Hitler accepts or rejects doctrines on political grounds, without bringing in the notion of truth or falsehood. Poor William James, who invented this point of view, would be horrified at the use which is made of it; but when once the conception of objective truth is abandoned, it is clear that the question 'what shall I believe?' is one to be settled, as I wrote in 1907, by 'the appeal to force and the arbitrament of the big battalions', not by the methods of either theology or science. States whose policy is based upon the revolt against reason must therefore find themselves in conflict, not only with learning, but also with the Churches wherever any genuine Christianity survives.

An important element in the causation of the revolt against reason is that many able and energetic men have no outlet for their love of power, and therefore become subversive. Small States, formerly, gave more men political power, and small businesses gave more men economic power. Consider the huge population that sleeps in suburbs and works in great cities. Coming into London by train, one passes through great regions of small villas, inhabited by families which feel no solidarity with the working class; the man of the family has no part in local affairs, since he is absent all day submitting to the orders of his employers; his only outlet for initiative is the cultivation of his back garden at the weekend. Politically, he is envious of all that is done for the working classes, but, though he feels poor, snobbery prevents him from adopting the methods of Socialism and trade unionism. His suburb may be as populous as many a famous city of antiquity, but its collective life is languid and he has no time to be interested in it. To such a man, if he has enough spirit for discontent, a Fascist movement may well appear as a deliverance.

The decay of reason in politics is a product of two factors: on the one hand, there are classes and types of individuals to whom the world as it is offers no scope, but who see no hope in Socialism because they are not wage-earners; on the other hand, there are able and powerful men whose interests are opposed to those of the community at large, and who, therefore, can best retain their influence by promoting various kinds of hysteria. Anti-Communism, fear of foreign armaments, and hatred of foreign competition, are the most important bogeys. I do not mean that no rational man could feel these sentiments; I mean that they are used in a way to preclude intelligent consideration of practical issues. The two things the world needs most are Socialism and peace, but both are contrary to the interests of the most powerful men of our time. It is not difficult to make the steps leading up to them *appear* contrary to the interests of large sections of the population, and the easiest way of doing this is to generate mass hysteria. The greater the danger of Socialism and peace the more Governments will debauch the mental life of their subjects; and the greater the economic hardships of the present, the more willing the sufferers will be to be seduced from intellectual sobriety in favour of some delusive will o' the wisp.

The fever of nationalism which has been increasing ever since 1848 is one form of the cult of unreason. The idea of one universal truth has been abandoned: there is English truth, French truth, German truth, Montenegran truth, and truth for the principality of Monaco. Similarly there is truth for the wage-earner and truth for the capitalist. Between these different 'truths', if rational persuasion is despaired of, the only possible decision is by means of war and rivalry in propagandist insanity. Until the deep conflicts of nations and classes which infect our world have been resolved, it is hardly to be expected that mankind will return to a rational habit of mind. The difficulty is that, so long as unreason prevails, a solution of our troubles can only be reached by chance; for while reason, being impersonal, makes universal co-operation possible, unreason, since it represents private passions, makes strife inevitable. It is for this reason that rationality, in the sense of an appeal to a universal and impersonal standard of truth, is of supreme importance to the well-being of the human species, not only in ages in which it easily prevails, but also, and even more, in those less fortunate times in which it is despised and rejected as the vain dream of men who lack the virility to kill where they cannot agree.

6

SCYLLA AND CHARYBDIS, OR COMMUNISM AND FASCISM

It is said by many in the present day that Communism and Fascism are the only practical alternatives in politics, and that whoever does not support the one in effect supports the other. I find myself in opposition to both, and I can no more accept either alternative than, if I had lived in the sixteenth century, I could have been either a Protestant or a Catholic. I will set forth, as briefly as I can, my objections, first to Communism, then to Fascism, and then to what both have in common.

When I speak of a 'Communist', I mean a person who accepts the doctrines of the Third International. In a sense, the early Christians were Communists, and so were many medieval sects; but this sense is now obsolete. I will set forth my reasons for not being a Communist *seriatim*.

1. I cannot assent to Marx's philosophy, still less to that of Lenin's *Materialism and Empirio-Criticism*. I am not a materialist, though I am even further removed from idealism. I do not believe that there is any dialectical necessity in historical change;

this belief was taken over by Marx from Hegel, without its only logical basis, namely, the primacy of the Idea. Marx believed that the next stage in human development must be in some sense a progress; I see no reason for this belief.

2. I cannot accept Marx's theory of value, nor yet, in his form, the theory of surplus value. The theory that the exchange value of a commodity is proportional to the labour involved in its production, which Marx took over from Ricardo, is shown to be false by Ricardo's theory of rent, and has long been abandoned by all non-Marxian economists. The theory of surplus value rests upon Malthus's theory of population, which Marx elsewhere rejects. Marx's economics do not form a logical coherent whole, but are built up by the alternate acceptance and rejection of older doctrines, as may suit his convenience in making out a case against the capitalists.

3. It is dangerous to regard any one man as infallible; the consequence is necessarily an over-simplification. The tradition of the verbal inspiration of the Bible has made men too ready to look for a Sacred Book. But this worship of authority is contrary to the scientific spirit.

4. Communism is not democratic. What it calls the 'dictatorship of the proletariat' is in fact the dictatorship of a small minority, who become an oligarchic governing class. All history shows that government is always conducted in the interests of the governing class, except in so far as it is influenced by fear of losing its power. This is the teaching, not only of history, but of Marx. The governing class in a Communist State has even more power than the capitalist class in a 'democratic' State. So long as it retains the loyalty of the armed forces, it can use its power to obtain for itself advantages quite as harmful as those of capitalists. To suppose that it will always act for the general good is mere foolish idealism, and is contrary to Marxian political psychology.

5. Communism restricts liberty, particularly intellectual liberty, more than any other system except Fascism. The complete

unification of both economic and political power produces a terrifying engine of oppression, in which there are no loopholes for exceptions. Under such a system progress would soon become impossible, since it is the nature of bureaucrats to object to all change except increase in their own power. All serious innovation is only rendered possible by some accident enabling unpopular persons to survive. Kepler lived by astrology, Darwin by inherited wealth, Marx by Engels's 'exploitation' of the pro-letariat of Manchester. Such opportunities of surviving in spite of unpopularity would be impossible under Communism.

6. There is in Marx, and in current Communist thought, an undue glorification of manual as against brain workers. The result has been to antagonise many brain workers who might otherwise have seen the necessity of Socialism, and without whose help the organisation of a Socialist State is scarcely pos-sible. The division of classes is put by Marxians, in practice even more than in theory, too low in the social scale.

7. The preaching of the class-war is likely to cause it to break out at a moment when the opposing forces are more or less evenly balanced, or even when the preponderance is on the side of the capitalists. If the capitalist forces preponderate, the result is an era of reaction. If the forces on both sides are roughly equal, the result, given modern methods of warfare, is likely to be the destruction of civilisation, involving the disappearance of both capitalism and Communism. I think that, where democracy exists, Socialists should rely upon persuasion, and should only use force to repel an illegal use of force by their opponents. By this method it will be possible for Socialists to acquire so great a preponderance that the final war may be brief, and not suf-ficiently serious to destroy civilisation.

8. There is so much hate in Marx and in Communism that Communists can hardly be expected, when victorious, to estab-lish a régime affording no outlet for malevolence. The argu-ments in favour of oppression are therefore likely to seem to the

victors stronger than they are, especially if the victory has resulted from a fierce and doubtful war. After such a war the victorious party are not likely to be in the mood for sane reconstruction. Marxists are too apt to forget that war has its own psychology, which is the result of fear, and is independent of the original cause of contention.

The view that the only practically possible choice is between Communism and Fascism seems to me definitely untrue in America, England, and France, and probably also in Italy and Germany. England had a period of Fascism under Cromwell, France under Napoleon, but in neither case was this a bar to subsequent democracy. Politically immature nations are not the best guides as to the political future.

My objections to Fascism are simpler than my objections to Communism, and in a sense more fundamental. The purpose of the Communists is one with which, on the whole, I am in agreement; my disagreement is as to means rather than ends. But in the case of the Fascists I dislike the end as much as the means.

Fascism is a complex movement; its German and Italian forms differ widely, and in other countries, if it spreads, it may assume still other shapes. It has, however, certain essentials, without which it would cease to be Fascism. It is antidemocratic, it is nationalistic, it is capitalistic, and it appeals to those sections of the middle class which suffer through modern developments and expect to suffer still more if Socialism or Communism becomes established. Communism, also, is anti-democratic, but only for a time, at least so far as its theoretical statements can be accepted as giving its real policy; moreover, it aims at serving the interests of wage-earners, who are a majority in advanced countries, and are intended by Communists to become the whole population. Fascism is anti-democratic in a more fundamental sense. It does not accept the greatest happiness of the greatest number as the right principle in statesmanship, but selects certain individuals, nations, and classes as 'the best', and as alone worthy of consideration. The remainder are to be compelled by force to serve the interests of the elect.

While Fascism is engaged in the struggle to acquire power, it has to make an appeal to a considerable section of the population. Both in Germany and in Italy, it arose out of Socialism, by rejecting whatever was anti-nationalistic in the orthodox programme. It took over from Socialism the idea of economic planning and of an increase in the power of the State, but the planning, instead of being for the benefit of the whole world, was to be in the interests of the upper and middle class in one country. And these interests it seeks to secure, not so much by increased efficiency, as by increased oppression, both of wage-earners and of unpopular sections of the middle class itself. In relation to the classes which lie outside the scope of its benevolence, it may, at best, achieve the kind of success to be found in a well-run prison; more than this it does not even wish to do.

The root objection to Fascism is its selection of a portion of mankind as alone important. The holders of power have, no doubt, made such a selection, in practice, ever since government was first instituted; but Christianity, in theory, has always recognised each human soul as an end in itself, and not a mere means to the glory of others. Modern democracy has derived strength from the moral ideals of Christianity, and has done much to divert Governments from exclusive preoccupation with the interests of the rich and powerful. Fascism is, in this respect, a return to what was worst in ancient paganism.

If Fascism could succeed, it would not do anything to cure the evils of capitalism; on the contrary, it would make them even worse. The manual work would come to be performed by forced labour at subsistence level; the men engaged in it would have no political rights, no freedom as to where they lived or worked, and probably not even a permanent family life; they would, in fact, be slaves. All this may already be seen beginning in the

German method of dealing with unemployment; it is, indeed, an inevitable result of capitalism freed from the control of democracy, and the similar conditions of forced labour in Russia suggest that it is an inevitable result of any dictatorship. In the past, absolutism has always been accompanied by some form of slavery or serfdom.

All this would result if Fascism were to succeed, but it is hardly possible that it should permanently succeed, because it cannot solve the problem of economic nationalism. The most powerful force on the side of the Nazis has been heavy industry, especially steel and chemicals. Heavy industry, organised nationally, is the greatest influence making for war in the present day. If every civilised country had a Government subservient to the interests of heavy industry—as is, to a considerable extent, already the case—war, before long, would be unavoidable. Each fresh victory of Fascism brings war nearer; and war, when it comes, is likely to sweep away Fascism along with most of what will have been in existence at its outbreak.

Fascism is not an ordered set of beliefs, like laisser-faire or Socialism or Communism; it is essentially an emotional protest, partly of those members of the middle class (such as small shopkeepers) who suffer from modern economic developments, partly of anarchic industrial magnates whose love of power has grown into megalomania. It is irrational, in the sense that it cannot achieve what its supporters desire; there is no philosophy of Fascism, but only a psycho-analysis. If it could succeed, the result would be widespread misery; but its inability to find a solution for the problem of war makes it impossible that it should succeed for more than a brief moment.

I do not think that England and America are likely to adopt Fascism, because the tradition of representative Government is too strong in both countries to permit such a development. The ordinary citizen has a feeling that public affairs concern him, and would not wish to lose the right of expressing his political opinions. General Elections and Presidential Elections are sporting events, like the Derby, and life would seem duller without them. Of France it is impossible to feel quite so confident. But I shall be surprised if France adopts Fascism, except perhaps temporarily during a war.

There are some objections—and these, to my mind, the most conclusive—which apply to Communism and Fascism equally. Both are attempts by a minority to mould a population forcibly in accordance with a preconceived pattern. They regard a population as a man regards the materials out of which he intends to construct a machine: the materials undergo much alteration, but in accordance with his purposes, not with any law of development inherent in them. Where living beings are concerned, and most of all in the case of human beings, spontaneous growth tends to produce certain results, and others can only be produced by means of a certain stress and strain. Embryologists may produce beasts with two heads, or with a nose where a toe should be; but such monstrosities do not find life very pleasant. Similarly Fascists and Communists, having in their minds a picture of society as a whole, distort individuals so as to make them fit into a pattern; those who cannot be adequately distorted are killed or placed in concentration camps. I do not think an outlook of this sort, which totally ignores the spontaneous impulses of the individual, is ethically justifiable, or can, in the long run, be politically successful. It is possible to cut shrubs into the shape of peacocks, and by a similar violence a similar distortion can be inflicted upon human beings. But the shrub remains passive, while the man, whatever the dictator may desire, remains active, if not in one sphere then in another. The shrub cannot pass on the lesson in the use of the shears which the gardener has been teaching, but the distorted human being can always find humbler human beings upon whom he can wield smaller shears. The inevitable effects of artificial moulding upon the individual are to produce either cruelty or listlessness, perhaps both in alternation. And from a population with these characteristics no good thing is to be expected.

The moral effect upon the Dictator is another matter to which both Communists and Fascists give insufficient consideration. If he is, to begin with, a man with little human sympathy, he will, from the first, be unduly ruthless, and will shrink from no cruelty in pursuit of his impersonal ends. If, initially, he suffers sympathetically from the misery which theory obliges him to inflict, he will either have to give way to a successor made of sterner stuff, or will have to stifle his humanitarian feelings, in which case he is likely to become even more sadistic than the man who has undergone no such struggle. In either case, government will be in the hands of ruthless men, in whom love of power will be camouflaged as desire for a certain type of society. By the inevitable logic of despotism, whatever of good may have existed in the original purposes of the dictatorship will gradually fade out of sight, and the preservation of the Dictator's power will emerge more and more as the naked purpose of the State machine.

Preoccupation with machines has produced what may be called the manipulator's fallacy, which consists in treating individuals and societies as if they were inanimate, and manipulators as if they were divine beings. Human beings change under treatment, and the operators themselves change as a result of the effect which the operations have upon them. Social dynamics is therefore a very difficult science, about which less is known than is necessary to warrant a dictatorship. In the typical manipulator, all feeling for natural growth in his patient is atrophied; the result is not, as he hopes, passive adaptation to a place in the preconceived pattern, but morbid and distorted growth, leading to a pattern which is grotesque and macabre. The ultimate psychological argument for democracy and for patience is that an element of free growth, of go as you please and untrained natural living, is essential if men are not to become misshapen monsters. In any case, believing, as I do, that Communist and Fascist dictatorships are alike undesirable, I deplore the tendency to view them as the only alternatives, and to treat democracy as obsolete. If men think them the only alternatives, they will become so; if men think otherwise, they will not.

7

THE CASE FOR SOCIALISM

The great majority of Socialists, in the present day, are disciples
of Karl Marx, from whom they have taken over the belief that the
only possible political force by which Socialism can be brought
about is the anger felt by the dispossessed proletariat against the
owners of the means of production. By an inevitable reaction,
those who are not proletarians have decided, with comparatively
few exceptions, that Socialism is something to be resisted; and
when they hear the class-war being preached by those who
proclaim themselves as their enemies, they naturally feel
inclined to begin the war themselves while they still hold the
power. Fascism is a retort to Communism, and a very formidable
retort. So long as Socialism is preached in Marxist terms, it
rouses such powerful antagonism that its success, in developed
Western countries, becomes daily more improbable. It would, of
course, have aroused opposition from the rich in any case, but
the opposition would have been less fierce and less widespread.

For my part, while I am as convinced a Socialist as the
most ardent Marxian, I do not regard Socialism as a gospel of

proletarian revenge, nor even, primarily, as a means of securing economic justice. I regard it primarily as an adjustment to machine production demanded by considerations of common sense, and calculated to increase the happiness, not only of proletarians, but of all except a tiny minority of the human race. If it cannot now be realised without a violent upheaval, this is to be attributed largely to the violence of its advocates. But I still have some hope that a saner advocacy may soften the opposition, and make a less catastrophic transition possible.

Let us begin by a definition of Socialism. The definition must consist of two parts, economic and political. The economic part consists in State ownership of ultimate economic power, which involves, as a minimum, land and minerals, capital, banking, credit and foreign trade. The political part requires that the ultimate political power should be democratic. Marx himself, and practically all Socialists before 1918, would have agreed to this part of the definition without question, but since the Bolsheviks dissolved the Russian Constituent Assembly, a different doctrine has grown up, according to which, when a Socialist Government has achieved success by revolution, only its most ardent supporters are to have political power. Now it must, of course, be admitted that, after a civil war, it is not always possible to enfranchise the vanquished immediately, but, in so far as this is the case, it is not possible to establish Socialism immediately. A Socialist Government which has carried out the economic part of Socialism will not have completed its task until it has secured enough popular support to make democratic government possible. The necessity of democracy is evident if we take an extreme case. An Oriental despot may decree that all the natural resources in his territory shall be his, but is not, in so doing, establishing a Socialist régime; nor can the rule of Leopold II in the Congo be accepted as a model for imitation. Unless there is popular control, there can be no reason to expect the State to conduct its economic enterprises except for its own enrichment, and therefore exploitation will merely take a new form. Democracy, accordingly, must be accepted as part of the definition of a Socialist régime.

With regard to the economic part of the definition, some further elucidation is necessary, since there are forms of private enterprise which some would consider compatible with Socialism while others would hold the opposite view. Should a pioneer be allowed to build himself a log hut on a piece of land rented from the State? Yes, but it does not follow that private individuals should be allowed to build skyscrapers in New York. Similarly, a man may lend a shilling to a friend, but a financier may not lend ten millions to a company or a foreign Government. The matter is one of degree, and is easy to adjust, since various legal formalities are necessary in large transactions, but not in small ones. Where such formalities are indispensable, they give the State opportunity to exercise control. To take another instance: jewellery is not capital in the economic sense, since it is not a means of production, but as things are a man who possesses diamonds can sell them and buy shares. Under Socialism he may still possess diamonds, but he cannot sell them to buy shares, since there will be no shares to be bought. Private wealth need not be legally prohibited, but only private investment, with the result, that, since no one will be in receipt of interest, private wealth will gradually melt away except as regards a reasonable modicum of personal possessions. Economic power over other human beings must not belong to individuals, but such private property as does not confer economic power may survive.

The advantages to be expected from the establishment of Socialism, supposing this to be possible without a devastating revolutionary war, are of many different kinds, and are by no means confined to the wage-earning class. I am far from confident that all or any of these advantages would result from the victory of a Socialist party in a long and difficult class conflict, which would exacerbate tempers, bring to the fore a ruthless militaristic type, waste by death or exile or imprisonment the talents of many valuable experts, and give to the victorious Government a barrackroom type of mentality. The merits which I shall claim for Socialism all presuppose that it will have been brought about by persuasion, and that such force as may be necessary will consist only of the defeat of small bands of malcontents. I am persuaded that, if Socialist propaganda were conducted with less hate and bitterness, appealing not to envy but to the obvious need of economic organisation, the task of persuasion would be enormously facilitated, and the need for force correspondingly diminished. I deprecate the appeal to force, except in defence of what, through persuasion, has become legally established, because (a) it is likely to fail, (b) the struggle must be disastrously destructive, and (c) the victors, after an obstinate fight, are likely to have forgotten their original objects, and to institute something quite different, probably a military tyranny. I presuppose, therefore, as a condition for successful Socialism, the peaceful persuasion of a majority to acceptance of its doctrines.

I shall adduce nine arguments in favour of Socialism, none of them new, and not all of equal importance. The list could be indefinitely lengthened, but I think these nine should suffice to show that it is not a gospel for one class only.

1 THE BREAKDOWN OF THE PROFIT MOTIVE

Profit, as a separate economic category, only becomes clear at a certain stage of industrial development. The germ of it, however, might be seen in the relations of Robinson Crusoe and his Man Friday. Let us suppose that, in the autumn, Robinson Crusoe, by means of his gun, has acquired control of the whole food supply of his island. He is then in a position to cause Friday to work at the preparation of next year's harvest, on the understanding that Friday shall be kept alive while all the surplus shall go to his employer. What Robinson Crusoe receives under this contract may be regarded as interest on his capital, his capital being his few tools and the stored-up food which he possesses. But profit, as it occurs in more civilised conditions, involves the further circumstance of exchange. A cotton manufacturer, for example, does not make cotton only for himself and his family; cotton is not the only thing he needs, and he has to sell the bulk of his produce in order to satisfy his other requirements. But before he can manufacture cotton he has to buy other things: raw cotton, machinery, labour, and power. His profit consists of the difference between what he pays for these things and what he receives for the finished product. But if he himself manages his factory, we must deduct whatever would have been the salary of a manager hired to do the same work; that is to say, the manufacturer's profit consists of his total earnings less the wages of the hypothetical manager. In large businesses, where the shareholders do no work of management, what they receive is the profit of the enterprise. Those who have money to invest are actuated by the expectation of profit, which is therefore the determining motive as to what new undertakings shall be started and what old ones shall be expanded. It has been supposed by the defenders of our present system that the expectation of profit would lead, on the whole, to the right commodities being produced in the right quantities. Up to a point, this has been true in the past, but it is true no longer.

This is a result of the complicated character of modern production. If I am an old-fashioned village cobbler, and the neighbours bring me their shoes to be mended, I know that the produce of my labour will be wanted; but if I am a large-scale manufacturer of shoes, employing expensive machinery, I have to guess how many pairs of shoes I shall be able to sell, and I may easily guess wrong. Another man may have better machinery, and be able to sell shoes more cheaply; or my former customers may have grown poorer, and have learnt to make old shoes last longer, or the fashion may change, and people may demand a kind of shoe which my machines are unable to produce. If any of these things happen, not only do I cease to make a profit but my machines stand idle and my employees are out of work. The labour that went into the making of my machines failed to result in the production of useful commodities, and was as completely wasted as if it had consisted of throwing sand into the sea. The men who are thrown out of employment are no longer creating anything that serves human needs, and the community is impoverished to the extent of whatever is spent on keeping them from starvation. The men, being dependent upon employment benefit instead of wages, spend much less than formerly, and therefore cause unemployment among those who make the goods which they formerly bought. And so the original miscalculation as to the number of shoes that I could sell at a profit produces gradually widening circles of unemployment, with accompanying diminution of demand. As for me, I am tethered to my expensive machinery, which has probably absorbed all my capital and credit; this makes it impossible for me to turn suddenly from shoes to some more prosperous industry.

Or take a more speculative business: ship-building. During the war, and for a little while afterwards, there was an immense demand for ships. As no one knew how long the war might last, or how successful the U-boats might be, enormously elaborate preparations were made for building unprecedented numbers of ships. By 1920, the war losses had been made good, and the need of ships, owing to the diminution of sea-borne trade, had suddenly grown much less. Almost all the ship-building plant became useless, and the great majority of the men employed were thrown out of work. It cannot be said that they deserved this misfortune, since the Governments had urged them frantically to build ships as fast as they could. But under our system of private enterprise the Governments had no recognised responsibility towards those who had been rendered destitute. And inevitably the destitution spread. There was less demand for steel, and therefore the iron and steel industry suffered. There was less demand for Australian and Argentine meat, because the unemployed had to be content with a spare diet. There was, as a result, less demand for the manufactures which Australia and the Argentine had taken in exchange for their meat. And so on indefinitely.

There is one further very important reason for the failure of the profit motive in the present day, and that is the failure of scarcity. It often happens that goods of certain kinds can be produced in enormous quantities at a cheaper rate than on a more modest scale. In that case, it may be that the most economical mode of production would be to have only one factory for each of these kinds of goods in the whole world. But as this state of affairs has come about gradually, there are in fact many factories. Each knows that if it were alone in the world it could supply everybody and make a large profit; but as it is, there are competitors, no one is working up to full capacity, and therefore no one is making a secure profit. This leads to economic imperialism, since the only possibility of profit lies in the exclusive control of some huge market. Meanwhile the weaker competitors go under, and the larger the units the greater is the dislocation when one of them closes down. Competition leads to so much being produced that it cannot be sold at a profit; but the reduction in the supply is unduly slow, since, where there is much expensive machinery, it may be less disastrous to produce for a term of years at a loss than not to produce at all.

All these confusions and dislocations result from leaving modern large-scale industry to be directed by the motive of private profit.

In a capitalistic régime, the cost which determines whether a certain product shall be manufactured by a certain firm is the cost to that firm, not to the community. Let us illustrate the difference by an imaginary example. Suppose someone—say

Mr Henry Ford—finds out a way of making motor-cars so cheaply that no one else can compete, with the result that all the other firms engaged in making cars go bankrupt. In order to arrive at the cost to the community of one of the new cheap cars, one must add, to what Mr Ford would have to pay, the proper proportion of all the now useless plant belonging to other firms, and of the cost of rearing and educating those workers and managers previously employed by other firms but now out of work. (Some will obtain employment with Mr Ford, but probably not all, since the new process is cheaper, and therefore requires less labour.) There may well also be other expenses to the community—labour disputes, strikes, riots, extra police, trials and imprisonments. When all these items are taken into account, it may well be found that the cost of the new cars to the community is, at first, considerably greater than that of the old ones. Now it is the cost to the community which determines what is socially advantageous, while the cost to the individual manufacturer which determines, in our system, what takes place.

How Socialism would deal with this problem I shall explain at a later stage.

2   THE POSSIBILITY OF LEISURE[1]

Owing to the productivity of machines, much less work than was formerly necessary is now needed to maintain a tolerable standard of comfort in the human race. Some careful writers maintain that one hour's work a day would suffice, but perhaps this estimate does not take sufficient account of Asia. I shall assume, in order to be quite sure of being on the safe side, that four hours' work a day on the part of all adults would suffice to

[1] I shall treat this topic briefly, since it is discussed in the first essay of this volume.

produce as much material comfort as reasonable people ought to desire.

At present, however, owing to the operation of the profit motive, leisure cannot be distributed evenly: some are over-worked, while others are wholly unemployed. This results as follows: the value of the wage-earner to the employer depends upon the amount of work he does, which, so long as the hours do not exceed seven or eight, is supposed by the employer to be proportional to the length of the working day. The wage-earner, on the other hand, prefers a rather long day at good wages to a very short one at much lower wages. Hence it suits both parties to have a long working day, leaving those who, in consequence, are unemployed to starve or to be cared for by the public author-ities at the public expense.

Since the majority of the human race do not, at present, reach a reasonable level of material comfort, an average of less than four hours' work a day, wisely directed, would suffice to pro-duce what is now produced in the way of necessaries and simple comforts. That means that, if the average working day for those who have work is eight hours, more than half the workers would be unemployed if it were not for certain forms of inefficiency and unnecessary production. To take first inefficiency: we have already seen some of the waste involved in competition, but we must add to this all that is spent in advertising and all the very skilled work that goes into marketing. Nationalism involves another kind of waste: American automobile manufacturers, for example, find it necessary, owing to tariffs, to establish works in the principal European countries, whereas it would obviously save labour if they could produce all their cars in one huge establishment in the United States. Then there is the waste involved in armaments, and in military training, which involves the whole male population wherever there is compulsory mili-tary service. Thanks to these and other forms of extravagance, together with the luxuries of the rich, more than half the population is still employed. But so long as our present system lasts, every step towards the elimination of waste can only make the plight of the wage-earners even worse than it is now.

3 ECONOMIC INSECURITY

In the present state of the world, not only are many people destitute, but the majority of those who are not are haunted by a perfectly reasonable fear that they may become so at any moment. Wage-earners have the constant danger of unemployment; salaried employees know that their firm may go bankrupt or find it necessary to cut down its staff; business men, even those who are reputed to be very rich, know that the loss of all their money is by no means improbable. Professional men have a very hard struggle. After making great sacrifices for the education of their sons and daughters, they find that there are not the openings that there used to be for those who have the kinds of skill that their children have acquired. If they are lawyers, they find that people can no longer afford to go to law, although serious injustices remain unremedied; if they are doctors, they find that their formerly lucrative hypochondriac patients can no longer afford to be ill, while many genuine sufferers have to forgo much-needed medical treatment. One finds men and women of university education serving behind the counters in shops, which may save them from destitution, but only at the expense of those who would formerly have been so employed. In all classes, from the lowest to almost the highest, economic fear governs men's thoughts by day and their dreams at night, making their work nerve-racking and their leisure unrefreshing. This ever-present terror is, I think, the main cause of the mood of madness which has swept over great parts of the civilised world.

The desire for wealth is, in most cases, due to a desire for security. Men save money and invest it, in the hope of having something to live on when they become old and infirm, and of being able to prevent their children from sinking in the social scale. In former days, this hope was rational, since there were such things as safe investments. But now security has become unattainable: the largest businesses fail, States go bankrupt, and whatever still stands is liable to be swept away in the next war. The result, except for those who continue to live in a fool's paradise, is a mood of unhappy recklessness, which makes a sane consideration of possible remedies very difficult.

Economic security would do more to increase the happiness of civilised communities than any other change that can be imagined, except the prevention of war. Work—to the extent that may be socially necessary—should be legally obligatory for all healthy adults, but their income should depend only upon their willingness to work, and should not cease when, for some reason, their services are temporarily unnecessary. A medical man, for example, should receive a certain salary, ceasing only with his death, though he would not be expected to work after a certain age. He should be sure of a good education for his children. If the health of the community improved so much that there was no longer need of the direct medical services of all qualified practitioners, some of them should be employed in medical research or in investigating measures of sanitation or the promotion of a more adequate diet. I do not think it can be doubted that the great majority of medical men would be happier under such a system than they are at present, even if it involved a diminution in the rewards of the few who achieve eminent success.

The desire for exceptional wealth is by no means a necessary stimulus to work. At present, most men work, not in order to be rich, but in order to avoid starvation. A postman does not expect to become richer than other postmen, nor does a soldier or sailor hope to amass a fortune by serving his country. There are a few men, it is true—and they tend to be men of exceptional energy and importance—to whom the achievement of a great financial success is a dominant motive. Some do good, others do harm; some make or adopt a useful invention, others manipulate the stock exchange or corrupt politicians. But in the main what they want is success, of which money is the symbol. If success were only obtainable in other forms, such as honours or important administrative posts, they would still have an adequate incentive, and might find it more necessary than they do now to work in ways advantageous to the community. The desire for wealth in itself, as opposed to the desire for success, is not a socially useful motive, any more than the desire for excess in eating or drinking. A social system is therefore none the worse for leaving no outlet to this desire. On the other hand, a system which abolished insecurity would do away with most of the hysteria of modern life.

4 THE UNEMPLOYED RICH

The evils of unemployment among wage-earners are generally recognised. The suffering to themselves, the loss of their labour to the community, and the demoralising effect of prolonged failure to find work are such familiar themes that it is unnecessary to enlarge upon them.

The unemployed rich are an evil of a different sort. The world is full of idle people, mostly women, who have little education, much money, and consequently great self-confidence. Owing to their wealth, they are able to cause much labour to be devoted to their comfort. Although they seldom have any genuine culture, they are the chief patrons of art, which is not likely to please them unless it is bad. Their uselessness drives them into an unreal sentimentality, which causes them to dislike vigorous sincerity, and to exercise a deplorable influence upon culture. Especially in America, where the men who make money are mostly too busy to spend it themselves, culture is largely dominated by women whose sole claim to respect is that their husbands possess the art of growing rich. There are those who maintain that capitalism is more favourable to art than Socialism would be, but I think they are remembering the aristocracies of the past and forgetting the plutocracies of the present.

The existence of the idle rich has other unfortunate results. Although, in the more important industries, the modern tendency is towards few large enterprises than many small ones, there are still many exceptions to this rule. Consider, for example, the number of unnecessary small shops in London. Throughout the parts where rich women do their shopping, there are innumerable hat shops, usually kept by Russian countesses, each professing to be a little more exquisite than any of the others. Their customers drift from one to the next, spending hours on a purchase which ought to be a matter of minutes. The labour of those who serve in the shops and the time of those who buy in them is alike wasted. And there is the further evil that the livelihood of a number of people becomes bound up with futility. The spending power of the very rich causes them to have large numbers of parasites who, however far removed from wealth they may be themselves, nevertheless fear that they would be ruined if there were no idle rich to buy their wares. All these people suffer morally, intellectually, and artistically from their dependence upon the indefensible power of foolish people.

5 EDUCATION

Higher education, at present, is mainly, though not entirely, confinded to the children of the well-to-do. It sometimes happens, it is true, that working-class boys or girls reach the university by means of scholarships, but as a rule they have had to work so hard in the process that they are worn out and do not fulfil their early promise. The result of our system is that there is a great waste of ability: a boy or girl born of wage-earning parents may be of first-rate capacity in mathematics, or music, or science, but it is very unlikely that he or she will have a chance to exercise this talent. Moreover, education, at least in England, is still infected through and through with snobbery: in private and elementary schools consciousness of class is imbibed by the pupils at every moment of their school life. And since education is, in the main, controlled by the State, it has to defend the *status quo*, and therefore must, as far as possible, blunt the critical faculties of young people and preserve them from 'dangerous thoughts'. All this, it must be admitted, is inevitable in any insecure régime, and is worse in Russia than in England or America. But while a Socialist régime might, in time, become sufficiently secure to be not afraid of criticism, it is now hardly possible that this should happen to a capitalistic régime, unless by the establishment of a slave State in which the workers receive no education at all. It is not to be expected, therefore, that the present defects in the educational system can be remedied until the economic system has been transformed.

6 THE EMANCIPATION OF WOMEN AND THE WELFARE OF YOUNG CHILDREN

In spite of all that has been done in recent times to improve the status of women, the great majority of wives are still financially dependent upon their husbands. Their dependence is in various ways worse than that of a wage-earner upon his employer. An employee can throw up his job, but for a wife this is difficult; moreover, however hard she has to work in keeping the house, she cannot claim money wages. So long as this state of affairs persists, it cannot be said that wives have anything approaching economic equality with men. Yet it is difficult to see how the matter can be remedied without the establishment of Socialism. It is necessary that the expense of children should be borne by the State rather than by the husband, and that married women, except during lactation and the latter part of pregnancy, should earn their living by work outside the home. This will require certain architectural reforms (considered in an earlier essay in this volume), and the establishment of nursery schools for very young children. For the children, as for their mothers, this will be a great boon, since children require conditions of space and light and diet which are impossible in a wage-earner's home, but can be provided cheaply in a nursery school.

A reform of this sort in the position of wives and the rearing of young children may be possible without complete Socialism, and has even been carried out here and there on a small scale and incompletely. But it cannot be carried out adequately and completely except as part of a general economic transformation of society.

7 ART

Of the improvement to be expected in architecture from the introduction of Socialism, I have already spoken. Painting, in former days, accompanied and adorned spacious architecture, and may do so again when the squalid privacy engendered by our competitive fear of our neighbours has given place to a desire for communal beauty. The modern art of the cinema has immense possibilities which cannot develop while the motive of producers is commercial; in fact, many are of opinion that the USSR has come nearest to realising these possibilities. How literature suffers from the commercial motive, every writer knows: almost all vigorous writing offends some group, and therefore makes sales less. It is difficult for writers not to measure their own merit by their royalties, and when bad work brings great pecuniary rewards it requires unusual firmness of character to produce good work and remain poor.

It must be admitted that Socialism *might* make matters even worse. Since publishing will be a State monopoly, it will be easy for the State to exercise an illiberal censorship. So long as there is violent opposition to the new régime, this will be almost unavoidable. But when the transition period is passed it may be hoped that books which the State is not willing to accept on their merits may be published if the author thinks it worth while to defray the expense by working overtime. Since the hours will be short, this will be no excessive hardship, but it will suffice to deter authors who are not seriously convinced that their books contain something of value. It is important that it should be *possible* to get a book published, but not that it should be very easy. Books at present exceed in quantity as much as they fall short in quality.

8 UNPROFITABLE PUBLIC SERVICES

Ever since civilised government began it has been recognised that there are some things which should be done, but cannot be left to the haphazard operation of the profit motive. The most important of these has been war: even those who are most persuaded of the inefficiency of State enterprise do not suggest that national defence should be farmed out to private contractors. But there are many other things that the public authorities have found it necessary to undertake, such as roads, harbours, lighthouses, parks in cities, and so on. A very large department of socialised activity, which has grown up during the last hundred years, is public health. At first, the fanatical adherents of *laisser-faire* objected, but the practical arguments were overwhelming. If the theory of private enterprise had been adhered to, all sorts of new ways of making fortunes would have become possible. A man suffering from plague might have gone to a publicity agent who would have sent out circulars to railway companies, theatres, etc., saying that the man contemplated dying on their premises unless a large sum were paid to his widow. But it was decided that quarantine and isolation should not be left to voluntary effort, since the benefit was general and the loss individual.

The increasing number and complexity of the public services has been one of the characteristic features of the past century. The most enormous of these is education. Before this was enforced universally by the State, there were various motives for such schools and universities as existed. There were pious foundations dating from the Middle Ages, and secular foundations, such as the Collège de France, established by enlightened renaissance monarchs; and there were charity schools for the favoured poor. None of these were run for profit. There were, however, schools run for profit: of these Dotheboys Hall and Salem House were samples. There still are schools run for profit, and though the existence of education authorities prevents them from copying the model of Dotheboys Hall, they are apt to rely upon their gentility rather than upon a high standard of scholastic attainment. On the whole, the profit motive has had little influence on education, and that little bad.

Even when the public authorities do not actually carry out the work, they find it necessary to control it. Street lighting may be done by a private company, but it must be done, whether profitable or not. Houses may be built by private enterprise, but the building is controlled by by-laws. In this case, it is now generally recognised that a much stricter regulation would be desirable. Unitary town-planning, such as Sir Christopher Wren projected for London after the Great Fire, might do away with the hideousness and squalor of slums and suburbs and make modern cities beautiful, healthy, and pleasant. This example illustrates another of the arguments against private enterprise in our highly mobile world. The areas to be considered as units are too large to be dealt with by even the greatest plutocrats. London, for example, must be considered as a whole, since a large percentage of its inhabitants sleep in one part and work in another. Some important questions, such as the St Lawrence waterway, involve vast interests spread over different parts of two countries; in such cases, even a single Government does not cover a sufficient area. Persons, goods, and power can all be transported much more easily than in former days, with the result that small localities have less self-sufficiency than they had when the horse was the quickest mode of locomotion. Power stations are acquiring such importance that, if they are left in private hands, a new kind of tyranny becomes possible, comparable to that of the mediaeval baron in his castle. It is obvious that a community which depends upon a power station cannot have tolerable economic security if the power station is free to exploit its monopolistic advantages to the full. The mobility of goods still causes dependence upon the railway; that of persons has partially returned to dependence upon the road. Railways and motorcars have made the separation of townships obsolete, and aeroplanes are having the same effect on national frontiers. In these ways, larger and larger areas, involving more and more public control, are rendered increasingly necessary by the progress of invention.

9 WAR

I come now to the last and strongest argument for Socialism, namely, the need for preventing war. I shall not waste time on the likelihood of war or on its harmfulness, since these may be taken for granted. I shall confine myself to two questions: (1) How far is the danger of war at the present time bound up with capitalism? (2) How far would the establishment of Socialism remove the danger?

War is an ancient institution, not brought into being originally by capitalism, although its causes were always mainly economic. It had in the past two main sources, the personal ambitions of monarchs, and the expansive adventurousness of vigorous tribes or nations. Such a conflict as the Seven Years War exhibits both features: in Europe it was dynastic, whereas in America and India it was a conflict of nations. The conquests of the Romans were largely due to direct personal pecuniary motives on the part of the generals and their legionaries. Pastoral peoples, such as the Arabs, the Huns, and the Mongols, have been repeatedly started upon a career of conquest by the insufficiency of their former grazing grounds. And at all times, except when a monarch could enforce his will (as in the Chinese and later Roman Empires), war has been facilitated by the fact that vigorous males, confident of victory, enjoyed it, while their females admired them for their prowess. Although war has travelled far from its primitive beginnings, these ancient motives still survive, and must be remembered by those who wish war to cease. Only international Socialism will afford a *complete* safeguard against war, but national Socialism in all the principal civilised countries would, as I shall try to show, enormously diminish its likelihood.

While the adventurous impulse towards war still exists in a section of the population of civilised countries, the motives producing a desire for peace are much stronger than at any time during the last few centuries. People know by bitter experience that the late war did not bring prosperity even to the victors. They realise that the next war is likely to cause a loss of life among civilians to which there has been nothing comparable in magnitude at any time, or in intensity since the Thiry Years War, and that this loss will probably be by no means confined to one side. They fear that capital cities may be destroyed and a whole continent lost to civilisation. The British, in particular, are aware that they have lost their age-long immunity from invasion. These considerations have produced in Great Britain a passionate desire for peace, and in most other countries a feeling of the same sort though perhaps less intense.

Why, in spite of all this, is there an imminent danger of war? The proximate cause, of course, is the harshness of the Versailles Treaty, with the consequent growth of militant nationalism in Germany. But a new war would probably only produce an even harsher treaty than that of 1919, leading to an even more virulent reaction on the part of the vanquished. Permanent peace cannot issue from this endless see-saw, but only from elimination of the causes of enmity between nations. In the present day, these causes are mainly to be found in the economic interests of certain sections, and are therefore only to be abolished by a fundamental economic reconstruction.

Let us take the iron and steel industry as the most important example of the way in which economic forces promote war. The essential fact is that, with modern technique, the cost of production per ton is less if a vast quantity is produced than it is if the output is smaller. Consequently there is a profit if the market is sufficiently large, but not otherwise. The United States steel industry, having a home market which far exceeds all others, has so far had little need to trouble itself with politics, beyond interfering, when necessary, to block schemes of naval disarmament. But the German, French, and British steel industries all have a smaller market than their technical needs demand. They could, of course, secure certain advantages by amalgamations, but to this also there are economic objections. A great part of the demand for steel is connected with preparations for war, and therefore the steel industry as a whole profits by nationalism and the increase of national armaments. Moreover, both the Comité des Forges and the German steel trust hope, by war, to crush their rivals instead of having to share profits with them; and as the expense of war will fall mainly on others, they reckon that they may find the result financially advantageous. Probably they are mistaken, but the mistake is one which is natural to bold and self-confident men intoxicated with power. The fact that the vitally important Lorraine ore is in territory formerly German but now French increases the hostility of the two groups, and serves as a constant reminder of what can be achieved by war. And naturally the Germans are the more aggressive, since the French already enjoy the spoils of the late war.

It would, of course, be impossible for the steel industry, and the other industries which have similar interests, to cause great nations to serve their purposes, if there were not impulses in the population to which they could appeal. In France and England they can appeal to fear, in Germany to resentment against injustice; and these motives, on both sides, are perfectly valid. But if the matter could be given calm consideration, it would be obvious to both sides that an equitable agreement would make everybody happier. There is no good reason why the Germans should continue to suffer injustice, nor, if the injustice were removed, would they still have any reasonable excuse for behaving so as to inspire fear in their neighbours. But whenever an effort is made to be calm and reasonable, propaganda intervenes, in the shape of appeals to patriotism and national honour. The world is in the condition of a drunkard anxious to reform, but surrounded by kind friends offering him drinks, and therefore perpetually relapsing. In this case, the kind friends are men who make money out of his unfortunate propensity, and the first step in his reformation must be to remove them. It is only in this sense that modern capitalism can be regarded as a cause of war: it is not the whole cause, but it provides an essential stimulus to the other causes. If it were no longer in existence, the absence of this stimulus would quickly cause men to see the absurdity of war, and to enter upon such equitable agreements as would make its future occurrence improbable.

The complete and final solution of the problem presented by the steel industry and others having similar interests is only to be found in international Socialism, that is to say, in their operation by an authority representing all the Governments concerned. But nationalisation in each of the leading industrial countries would probably suffice to remove the pressing danger of war. For if the management of the steel industry were in the hands of the Government, and the Government were democratic, it would be conducted, not for its own benefit, but for the benefit of the nation. In the balance sheet of the public finances, profits made by the steel industry at the expense of other parts of the community would be offset by losses elsewhere, and as no individual's income would fluctuate with the gains or losses of one separate industry, no one would have any motive in pushing the interest of steel at the public expense. The increased production of steel due to an increase of armaments would appear as a loss, since it would diminish the supply of consumable commodities to be distributed among the population. In this way public and private interests would be harmonised, and the motive for deceptive propaganda would disappear.

It remains to say something as to the way in which Socialism would remedy the other evils we have been considering.

In place of the pursuit of profits as the guiding motive in industry, there will be Government planning. While the Government may miscalculate, it is less likely to do so than a private individual, because it will have fuller knowledge. When the price of rubber was high, everybody who could planted rubber trees, with the result that, after a few years, the price fell disastrously, and it was found necessary to make an agreement restricting the output of rubber. A central authority, which possesses all the statistics, can prevent this sort of miscalculation. Nevertheless, unforeseen causes, such as new inventions, may falsify even the most careful estimates. In such cases, the community as a whole gains by making the transition to new processes a gradual one. And in regard to those who, at any moment, are unemployed, it will be possible under Socialism to adopt measures which at present are impossible owing to the fear of unemployment and the mutual suspicions of employers and employed. When one industry is decaying and another expanding, the younger men can be taken out of the decaying industry and trained in the expanding one. Most of the unemployment can be prevented by shortening the hours of labour. When no work can be found for a man, he will receive full wages none the less, since he will be paid for willingness to work. In so far as work has to be enforced, it will be enforced by the criminal law, not by economic sanctions.

It will be left to those who do the planning, and therefore ultimately to the popular vote, to strike a balance between comfort and leisure. If everyone works four hours a day there will be less comfort than if everybody works five. One may expect that technological improvements will be utilised partly to provide more comfort and partly to provide more leisure.

Economic insecurity will no longer exist (except in so far as there may still be danger of war), since everyone will receive a salary so long as he is not a criminal, and the expense of children will be borne by the State. Wives will not be dependent upon husbands, nor will children be allowed to suffer seriously for their parents' defects. There will be no economic dependence of one individual upon another, but only of all individuals upon the State.

While Socialism exists in some civilised countries but not in others, there will still be a possibility of war, and the full benefits of the system will not be realisable. But I think it may be safely assumed that each country which adopts Socialism will cease to be aggressively militaristic, and will be genuinely concerned only to prevent aggression on the part of others. When Socialism has become universal throughout the civilised world, the motives for large-scale wars will probably no longer have sufficient force to overcome the very obvious reasons for preferring peace.

Socialism, I repeat, is not a doctrine for the proletariat only. By preventing economic insecurity, it is calculated to increase the happiness of all but a handful of the richest people; and if, as I firmly believe, it can prevent first-class wars, it will immeasurably increase the well-being of the whole world—for the belief of certain industrial magnates that they could profit by another

Great War, in spite of the economic argument by which their view can be made to seem plausible, is an insane delusion of megalomaniacs.

Is it really the case, as Communists maintain, that Socialism, a system so universally beneficient and so easy to understand, a system, moreover, recommended by the obvious breakdown of the present economic régime and by the pressing danger of universal disaster through war—is it really the case that this system cannot be presented persuasively except to proletarians and a handful of intellectuals, and can only be introduced by means of a bloody, doubtful, and destructive class-war? I, for my part, find this impossible to believe. Socialism, in some respects, runs counter to ancient habits, and therefore rouses an impulsive opposition which can only be overcome gradually. And in the minds of its opponents it has become associated with atheism and a reign of terror. With religion Socialism has nothing to do. It is an economic doctrine, and a Socialist might be a Christian or a Mohammedan, a Buddhist or a worshipper of Brahma, without any logical inconsistency. As for the reign of terror, there have been many reigns of terror in recent times, mostly on the side of reaction, and where Socialism comes as a revolt against one of these it is to be feared that it will inherit some of the fierceness of the previous régime. But in countries which still permit some degree of free thought and free speech, I believe that the Socialist case can, with ardour and patience combined, be so presented as to persuade much more than half the population. If, when that time comes, the minority illegally appeals to force, the majority will, of course, have to use force to suppress the rebels. But if the previous work of persuasion has been adequately performed, rebellion ought to be so obviously hopeless that even the most reactionary would not attempt it, or, if they did, they would be defeated so easily and quickly that there would be no occasion for a reign of terror. While persuasion is possible and a majority are still unpersuaded, the appeal to force is out of place; when a majority have been persuaded, the matter can be left to the ordinary operation of democratic government, unless lawless persons see fit to raise an insurrection. The suppression of such an insurrection would be a measure such as any Government would undertake, and Socialists have no more occasion to appeal to force than have other constitutional parties in democratic countries. And if Socialists are ever to have force at their command, it is only by previous persuasion that they can acquire it.

It is customary in certain circles to argue that, while Socialism might, perhaps at one time, have been secured by the ordinary methods of political propaganda, the growth of Fascism has now made this impossible. As regards the countries that have Fascist Governments this is, of course, true, since no constitutional opposition is possible. But in France, Great Britain, and the United States the matter is otherwise. In France and Great Britain there are powerful Socialist parties; in Great Britain and America the Communists are numerically negligible, and there is no sign that they are gaining ground. They have just sufficed to provide the reactionaries with an excuse for mildly repressive measures, but these have not been sufficiently terrifying to prevent the revival of the Labour Party or the growth of radicalism in the United States. It is far from improbable that Socialists will soon be in a majority in Great Britain. They will then, no doubt, encounter difficulties in carrying out their policy, and the more timid may try to make these difficulties an excuse for postponement, mistakenly, for, while persuasion, unavoidably, is gradual, the final transition to Socialism must be swift and sudden. But there is as yet no good ground for supposing that constitutional methods will fail, and there is much less for supposing that any others have a better chance of success. On the contrary, every appeal to unconstitutional violence helps on the growth of Fascism. Whatever may be the weaknesses of democracy, it is only by means of it and by the help of the popular belief in it that

Socialism can hope to succeed in Great Britain or America. Whoever weakens the respect for democratic government, is intentionally or unintentionally, increasing the likelihood, not of Socialism or Communism, but of Fascism.

8

WESTERN CIVILISATION

To see one's civilisation in a true perspective is by no means easy. There are three obvious means to this end, namely travel, history, and anthropology, and what I shall have to say is suggested by all three; but no one of the three is as great a help to objectivity as it appears to be. The traveller sees only what interests him; for example, Marco Polo never noticed Chinese women's small feet. The historian arranges events in patterns derived from his pre-occupations: the decay of Rome has been variously ascribed to imperialism, Christianity, malaria, divorce, and immigration—the last two being the favourites in America with parsons and politicians respectively. The anthropologist selects and interprets facts according to the prevailing prejudices of his day. What do we, who stay at home, know about the savage? Rousseauites say he is noble, imperialists say he is cruel; ecclesiastically minded anthropologists say he is a virtuous family man, while advocates of divorce law reform say he practises free love; Sir James Fraser says he is always killing his god, while others say he is always engaged in initiation ceremonies. In short, the savage is an obliging fellow who does whatever is necessary for the anthropologist's theories. In spite of these drawbacks, travel, history, and anthropology are the best means, and we must make the most of them.

First of all, what is civilisation? Its first essential character, I should say, is *forethought*. This, indeed, is what mainly distinguishes men from brutes and adults from children. But forethought being a matter of degree, we can distinguish more or less civilised nations and epochs according to the amount of it that they display. And forethought is capable of almost precise measurement. I will not say that the average forethought of a community is inversely proportional to the rate of interest, though this is a view which might be upheld. But we can say that the degree of forethought involved in any act is measured by three factors; present pain, future pleasure, and the length of the interval between them. That is to say, the forethought is obtained by dividing the present pain by the future pleasure and then multiplying by the interval of time between them. There is a difference between individual and collective forethought. In an aristocratic or plutocratic community, one man can endure the present pain while another enjoys the future pleasure. This makes collective forethought easier. All the characteristic works of industrialism exhibit a high degree of collective forethought in this sense: those who make railways, or harbours, or ships, are doing something of which the benefit is only reaped years later.

It is true no one in the modern world shows as much forethought as the ancient Egyptians showed in embalming their dead, for this was done with a view to their resurrection after some 10,000 years. This brings me to another element which is essential to civilisation, namely *knowledge*. Forethought based upon superstition cannot count as fully civilised, although it may bring habits of mind essential to the growth of true civilisation. For instance, the Puritan habit of postponing pleasures to the next life undoubtedly facilitated the accumulation of capital required for industrialism. We may then define civilisation as: *A manner of life due to the combination of knowledge and forethought*.

Civilisation in this sense begins with agriculture and the domestication of ruminants. There was until fairly recent times a sharp separation between agricultural and pastoral peoples. We read in Genesis xlvi. 31–4, how the Israelites had to settle in the land of Goshen rather than in Egypt proper because the Egyptians objected to pastoral pursuits: 'And Joseph said unto his brethren, and unto his father's house, I will go up, and shew Pharaoh, and say unto him, my brethren, and my father's house, which were in the land of Canaan, are come unto me; and the men are shepherds, for their trade hath been to feed cattle; and they have brought their flocks, and their herds, and all that they have. And it shall come to pass, when Pharaoh shall call you, and shall say, What is your occupation? That ye shall say, Thy servants' trade hath been about cattle from our youth even until now, both we, and also our fathers: that ye may dwell in the land of Goshen; for every shepherd is an abomination unto the Egyptians'. In the travels of M. Huc one finds a similar attitude of the Chinese towards the pastoral Mongols. On the whole, the agricultural type has always represented the higher civilisation, and has had more to do with religion. But the flocks and herds of the patriarchs had a considerable influence upon Jewish religion, and thence upon Christianity. The story of Cain and Abel is a piece of progapanda intended to show that shepherds are more virtuous than ploughmen. Nevertheless, civilisation rested mainly upon agriculture until quite modern times.

So far we have not considered anything that distinguishes Western civilisation from that of other regions such as India, China, Japan, and Mexico. There was in fact very much less difference before the rise of science than there has come to be since. Science and industrialism are nowadays the distinctive marks of Western civilisation; but I wish first to consider what our civilisation was before the Industrial Revolution.

If we go back to the origins of Western civilisation, we find that what it has derived from Egypt and Babylonia is, in the main, characteristic of all civilisations and not specially distinctive of the West. The distinctive Western character begins with the Greeks, who invented the habit of deductive reasoning and the science of geometry. Their other merits were either not distinctive or lost in the Dark Ages. In literature and art they may have been supreme, but they did not differ very profoundly from various other ancient nations. In experimental science they produced a few men, notably Archimedes, who anticipated modern methods, but these men did not succeed in establishing a school or a tradition. The one prominent distinctive contribution of the Greeks to civilisation was deductive reasoning and pure mathematics.

The Greeks, however, were politically incompetent, and their contribution to civilisation would probably have been lost but for the governmental capacity of the Romans. The Romans discovered how to carry on the government of a great empire by means of a civil service and a body of law. In previous empires everything had depended upon the vigour of the monarch, but in the Roman Empire the emperor could be murdered by the Praetorian Guards and the empire put up to auction with very little disturbance of the governmental machine—almost as little, in fact, as is now involved in a general election. The Romans seems to have invented the virtue of devotion to the impersonal State as opposed to loyalty to the person of the ruler. The Greeks, it is true, talked of patriotism, but their politicians were corrupt, and almost all of them at some period of their career accepted bribes from Persia. The Roman conception of devotion to the State has been an essential element in the production of stable government in the West.

One thing more was necessary to complete Western civilisation as it existed before modern times, and that was the peculiar relation between government and religion which came through

Christianity. Christianity was originally quite non-political, since it grew up in the Roman Empire as a consolation to those who had lost national and personal liberty; and it took over from Judaism an attitude of moral condemnation towards the rulers of the world. In the years before Constantine, Christianity developed an organisation to which the Christian owed a loyalty even greater than that which he owed to the State. When Rome fell, the Church preserved in a singular synthesis what had proved most vital in the civilisations of the Jews, the Greeks, and the Romans. From Jewish moral fervour came the ethical precepts of Christianity; from the Greek love of deductive reasoning came theology; from the example of Roman imperialism and jurisprudence came the centralised government of the Church and the body of Canon Law.

Although these elements of a high civilisation were, in a sense, preserved throughout the Middle Ages, they remained for a long time more or less latent. And Western civilisation was not in fact the best in existence at that time: both the Mohammedans and the Chinese were superior to the West. Why the West should have started upon such a rapid upward course is, I think, to a very great extent a mystery. It is customary in our age to find economic causes for everything, but explanations based upon this practice tend to be unduly facile. Economic causes alone will not, for example, explain the decay of Spain, which is attributable rather to intolerance and stupidity. Nor will economic causes explain the rise of science. The general rule is that civilisations decay except when they come in contact with an alien civilisation superior to their own. There have been only a few very rare periods in human history, and a few very sparse regions, in which spontaneous progress has occurred. There must have been spontaneous progress in Egypt and Babylonia when they developed writing and agriculture; there was spontaneous progress in Greece for about 200 years; and there has been spontaneous progress in Western Europe since the renaissance. But I do not think there has been anything in the general social conditions at these periods and places to distinguish them from various other periods and places in which no progress has occurred. I cannot escape from the conclusion that the great ages of progress have depended upon a small number of individuals of transcendent ability. Various social and political conditions were of course *necessary* for their effectiveness, but not *sufficient*, for the conditions have often existed without the individuals, and in such cases progress has not occurred. If Kepler, Galileo, and Newton had died in infancy, the world in which we live would be vastly less different than it is from the world of the sixteenth century. This carries with it the moral that we cannot regard progress as assured: if the supply of eminent individuals should happen to fail, we should no doubt lapse into a condition of Byzantine immobility.

There is one thing of great importance that we owe to the Middle Ages, and that is representative government. This institution is important because it has for the first time made it possible that the government of a large empire should appear to the governed to have been chosen by themselves. Where this system succeeds it produces a very high degree of political stability. It has, however, become evident in recent times that representative government is not a panacea applicable to all parts of the earth's surface. Indeed its success seems to be mainly confined to the English-speaking nations and the French.

Political cohesion by one mean or another has, nevertheless, become the distinctive mark of Western civilisation as opposed to the civilisations of other regions. This is mainly due to patriotism, which, although it has its roots in Jewish particularism and Roman devotion to the State, is a very modern growth, beginning with the English resistance to the Armada, and finding its first literary expression in Shakespeare. Political cohesion based mainly upon patriotism has been increasing steadily in the West ever since the end of the wars of religion, and is still increasing rapidly. In this respect Japan has proved an extraordinarily apt pupil. In old Japan there were turbulent feudal barons, analogous to those who infested England during the Wars of the Roses. But by the help of firearms and gunpowder, which were brought to Japan by the ships that brought the Christian missionaries, the Shogun established internal peace; and since 1868, by means of education and the Shinto religion, the Japanese Government has succeeded in producing a nation as homogeneous and resolute and united as any nation of the West.

The greater degree of social cohesion of the modern world is very largely due to changes in the art of war, all of which, from the invention of gunpowder onwards, have tended to increase the power of Governments. This process is probably by no means ended, but it has become complicated by a new factor: as armed forces become increasingly dependent upon industrial workers for their munitions, it becomes increasingly necessary for Governments to secure the support of large sections of the population. This is a matter belonging to the technique of propaganda, in which it may be assumed that Governments will make rapid progress in the near future.

The history of the last four hundred years in Europe has been one of simultaneous growth and decay: decay of the old synthesis represented by the Catholic Church, and growth of a new synthesis, as yet very incomplete, based hitherto on patriotism and science. It cannot be assumed that a scientific civilisation transplanted to regions that have not our antecedents will have the same features that it has among us. Science grafted upon Christianity and democracy may produce effects entirely different from those that it produces when grafted upon ancestor worship and absolute monarchy. We owe to Christianity a certain respect for the individual, but this is a feeling towards which science is entirely neutral. Science of itself does not offer us any moral ideas, and it is doubtful what moral ideas are going to replace those that we owe to tradition. Tradition changes slowly, and our moral ideas are still in the main those that were appropriate to a pre-industrial régime; but it cannot be expected that this will continue to be the case. Gradually men will come to have thoughts that will be in conformity with their physical habits, and ideals not inconsistent with their industrial technique. The rate of change in ways of life has become very much more rapid than in any previous period: the world has changed more in the last one hundred and fifty years than in the previous four thousand. If Peter the Great could have had a conversation with Hammurabi they would have understood each other fairly well; but neither of them could have understood a modern financial or industrial magnate. It is a curious fact that the new ideas of modern times have almost all been technical or scientific. Science has only lately begun to foster the growth of new moral ideas, through the liberation of benevolence from the shackles of superstitious ethical beliefs. Wherever a conventional code prescribes the infliction of suffering (e.g. in the prohibition of birth control), a kindlier ethic is thought to be immoral; consequently those who allow knowledge to influence their ethics are held by the apostles of ignorance to be wicked. It is, however, very doubtful whether a civilisation so dependent upon science as ours is can, in the long run, successfully prohibit forms of knowledge which are capable of greatly increasing human happiness.

The fact is that our traditional moral ideas are either purely individualistic, like the idea of personal holiness, or adapted to much smaller groups than those that are important in the modern world. One of the most noteworthy effects of modern technique upon social life has been the greater degree to which men's activities are organised into large groups, so that a man's acts have often a great effect upon some quite remote set of men with whom a group to which he belongs has relations of co-operation or conflict. Small groups, such as the family, are diminishing in importance, and there is only one large group, namely the nation or the State, of which traditional morality takes any account. The result is that the effective religion of our age, in so far as it is not *merely* traditional, consists of patriotism. The average man is willing to sacrifice his life to patriotism, and feels this moral obligation so imperative that no revolt appears to him possible.

It seems not improbable that the movement towards individual liberty which characterised the whole period from the renaissance to nineteenth-century liberalism may be brought to a stop by the increased organisation due to industrialism. The pressure of society upon the individual may, in a new form, become as great as in barbarous communities, and nations may come increasingly to pride themselves upon collective rather than individual achievements. This is already the case in the United States: men are proud of skyscrapers, railway stations, and bridges, rather than of poets, artists, or men of science. The same attitude pervades the philosophy of the Soviet Government. It is true that, in both countries, a desire for individual heroes persists: in Russia, personal distinction belongs to Lenin; in America, to athletes, pugilists, and movie stars. But in both cases the heroes are either dead or trivial, and the serious work of the present is not thus associated with the names of eminent individuals.

It is an interesting speculation to consider whether anything of high value can be produced by collective rather than individual effort, and whether such a civilisation can be of the highest quality. I do not think this question can be answered off-hand. It is possible that, both in matters of art and in matters of the intellect, better results will be achieved co-operatively than have in the past been achieved by individuals. In science, there is already a tendency for work to be associated with a laboratory rather than a single person, and it would probably be good for science if this tendency became more marked, since it would promote co-operation. But if important work, of whatever sort, is to be collective, there will of necessity be a certain curtailment of the individual: he will no longer be able to be so self-assertive as men of genius have usually been hitherto. Christian morality enters into this problem, but in an opposite sense to that usually supposed. It is generally thought that, because Christianity urges altruism and love of one's neighbour, it is anti-individualistic. This, however, is a psychological error. Christianity appeals to the individual soul, and emphasises personal salvation. What a man does for his neighbour, he has to do because that is what is right for him to do, not because he is instinctively part of a larger group. Christianity in its origin, and still in its essence, is not political, or even familial, and tends accordingly to make the individual more self-contained than nature made him. In the past, the family acted as a corrective to this individualism, but the family is decaying, and has not the hold over men's instincts that it used to have. What the family has lost, the nation has gained, for the appeal of the nation is to biological instincts which find little scope in an industrial world. From the point of view of stability, however, the nation is too narrow a unit. One could wish that men's biological instincts would apply themselves to the human race, but this seems hardly feasible psychologically, unless mankind as a whole is threatened by some grave external danger, such as a new disease or universal famine. These things being unlikely, I do not see any psychological mechanism by which world government could be brought about, except the conquest of the whole world by some one nation or group of nations. This does seem to be quite in the natural line of development, and may perhaps come about during the next one or two hundred years. In Western civilisation, such as it is now, science and industrial technique have much more importance than all the traditional factors put together. And it must not be supposed that the effect of these novelties upon human life has developed to anything like its full extent: things move more quickly now than they did in past ages, but they do not move so quickly as all that. The last event in human development comparable in importance to the growth of industrialism was the invention of agriculture, and agriculture took many thousands of years to spread over the earth's surface, carrying with it, as it spread, a system of ideas and a way of life. The agricultural way of life has not even yet wholly conquered the aristocracies of the world, which, with characteristic conservatism, have remained largely in the hunting stage, as is evidenced by our game laws. Similarly we may expect the agricultural outlook to survive for many ages in backward countries and in backward sections of the population.

But it is not this outlook that is distinctive of Western civilisation, or of the offspring to which it is giving birth in the East. In America one finds even agriculture associated with a semi-industrial mentality, because America has not an indigenous peasantry. In Russia and China, the government has an industrial outlook, but has to contend with a vast population of ignorant peasants. In this connection, however, it is important to remember that a population which cannot read or write can be more quickly transformed by government action than a population such as one finds in Western Europe or America. By producing literacy and supplying the right kind of propaganda, the State can lead the rising generation to despise its elders to an extent which would astonish the most advanced American flapper; and thus a very complete change of mentality can be brought about within a generation. In Russia this process is in full swing; in China it is beginning. These two countries may therefore be expected to develop an unadulterated industrial mentality freed from those traditional elements which have survived in the more slowly developing West.

Western civilisation has changed and is changing with such rapidity that many who feel an affection for its past find themselves living in what seems an alien world. But the present is only bringing out more clearly elements which have been present at any rate since Roman times, and which have always distinguished Europe from India and China. Energy, intolerance, and abstract intellect have distinguished the best ages in Europe from the best ages in the East. In literature and art, the Greeks may have been supreme, but their superiority to China is only a matter of degree. Of energy and intelligence I have already said enough; but of intolerance it is necessary to say something, since it has been a more persistent characteristic of Europe than many people realise.

The Greeks, it is true, were less addicted to this vice than their successors. Yet they put Socrates to death; and Plato, in spite of his admiration for Socrates, held that the State should teach a religion which he himself regarded as false, and that men should be persecuted for throwing doubt upon it. Confucians, Taoists, and Buddhists would not have sanctioned such a Hitlerite doctrine. Plato's gentlemanly elegance was not typically European; Europe has been warlike and clever, rather than urbane. The distinctive note of Western civilisation is rather to be found in Plutarch's account of the defence of Syracuse by mechanical contrivances invented by Archimedes.

One source of persecution, namely democratic envy, was well developed among the Greeks. Aristides was ostracised because his reputation for justice was annoying. Heraclitus of Ephesus, who was not a democrat exclaimed: 'The Ephesians would do well to hang themselves, every grown man of them, and leave the city to beardless lads; for they have cast out Hermodorus, the best man among them, saying, "We will have none who is best among us: if there be any such, let him be so elsewhere and among others".' Many of the unpleasant features of our age existed among the Greeks. They had Fascism, nationalism, militarism, Communism, bosses and corrupt politicians; they had pugnacious vulgarity and some religious persecution. They had good individuals, but so have we; then, as now, a considerable percentage of the best individuals suffered exile, imprisonment, or death. Greek civilisation had, it is true, one very real superiority to ours, namely the inefficiency of the police, which enabled a larger proportion of decent people to escape.

It was the conversion of Constantine to Christianity that first gave occasion for the full expression of those persecuting impulses by which Europe has distinguished itself from Asia. During the last hundred and fifty years, it is true, there has been a brief interval of liberalism, but now the white races are reverting to the theological bigotry which the Christians took over from the Jews. The Jews first invented the notion that only one religion could be true, but they had no wish to convert all the world to it, and therefore only persecuted other Jews. The Christians, retaining the Judaic belief in a special revelation, added to it the Roman desire for worldwide dominion and the Greek taste for metaphysical subtleties. The combination produced the most fiercely persecuting religion that the world has yet known. In Japan and China, Buddhism was peaceably accepted and allowed to exist along with Shinto and Confucianism; in the Mohammedan world, Christians and Jews were not molested so long as they paid the tribute; but throughout Christendom death was the usual penalty for even the smallest deviation from orthodoxy.

With those who dislike the intolerance of Fascism and Communism I have no disagreement, unless they regard it as a departure from European tradition. Those of us who feel stifled in an atmosphere of persecuting governmental orthodoxy would have fared little better in most previous ages of Europe than in modern Russia or Germany. If we could be transported into the past by magic, should we find Sparta an improvement on those modern countries? Should we have liked to live in societies which, like those of Europe in the sixteenth century, put men to death for not believing in the occurrence of witchcraft? Could we have endured early New England, or admired Pizarro's treatment of the Incas? Should we have enjoyed Renaissance

Germany, where 100,000 witches were burnt in a century? Should we have liked eighteenth-century America, where leading Boston divines attributed earthquakes in Massachusetts to the impiety of lightning-rods? In the nineteenth century, should we have sympathised with Pope Pius IX when he refused to have anything to do with the Society for the Prevention of Cruelty to Animals on the ground that it is heretical to believe that man has any duties to the lower animals? I am afraid Europe, however intelligent, has always been rather horrid, except in the brief period between 1848 and 1914. Now, unfortunately, Europeans are reverting to type.

9

ON YOUTHFUL CYNICISM

Any person who visits the Universities of the Western world is liable to be struck by the fact that the intelligent young of the present day are cynical to a far greater extent than was the case formerly. This is not true of Russia, India, China, or Japan; I believe it is not the case in Czechoslovakia, Jugoslavia, and Poland, nor by any means universally in Germany, but it certainly is a notable characteristic of intelligent youth in England, France, and the United States. To understand why youth is cynical in the West, we must also understand why it is not cynical in the East.

Young men in Russia are not cynical because they accept, on the whole, the Communist philosophy, and they have a great country full of natural resources, ready to be exploited by the help of intelligence. The young have therefore a career before them which they feel to be worth while. You do not have to consider the ends of life when in the course of creating Utopia you are laying a pipeline, building a railway, or teaching peasants to use Ford tractors simultaneously on a four-mile front.

Consequently the Russian youth are vigorous and filled with ardent beliefs.

In India the fundamental belief of the earnest young is in the wickedness of England: from this premiss, as from the existence of Descartes, it is possible to deduce a whole philosophy. From the fact that England is Christian, it follows that Hinduism or Mohammedanism, as the case may be, is the only true religion. From the fact that England is capitalistic and industrial, it follows, according to the temperament of the logician concerned, either that everybody ought to spin with a spinning-wheel, or that protective duties ought to be imposed to develop native industrialism and capitalism as the only weapons with which to combat those of the British. From the fact that the British hold India by physical force, it follows that only moral force is admirable. The persecution of nationalist activities in India is just sufficient to make them heroic, and not sufficient to make them seem futile. In this way the Anglo-Indians save the intelligent youth of India from the blight of cynicism.

In China hatred of England has also played its part, but a much smaller part than in India because the English have never conquered the country. The Chinese youth combine patriotism with genuine enthusiasm for Occidentalism, in the kind of way that was common in Japan fifty years ago. They want the Chinese people to be enlightened, free and prosperous, and they have their work cut out to produce this result. Their ideals are, on the whole, those of the nineteenth century, which in China has not yet begun to seem antiquated. Cynicism in China was associated with the officials of the Imperial régime and survived among the warring militarists who have distracted the country since 1911, but it has no place in the mentality of the modern intellectuals.

In Japan the outlook of young intellectuals is not unlike that which prevailed on the Continent of Europe between 1815 and 1848. The watchwords of Liberalism are still potent; parliamentary government, liberty of the subject, free thought and free speech. The struggle against traditional feudalism and autocracy is quite sufficient to keep young men busy and enthusiastic.

To the sophisticated youth of the West all this ardour seems a trifle crude. He is firmly persuaded that having studied everything impartially, he has seen through everything and found that there is 'nothing left remarkable beneath the visiting moon'. There are, of course, plenty of reasons for this in the teachings of the old. I do not think these reasons go to the root of the matter, for in other circumstances the young react against the teaching of the old and achieve a gospel of their own. If the Occidental youth of the present day react only by cynicism, there must be some special reason for this circumstance. Not only are the young unable to believe what they are told, but they seem also unable to believe anything else. This is a peculiar state of affairs, which deserves investigation. Let us first take some of the old ideals one by one and see why they no longer inspire the old loyalties. We may enumerate among such ideals: religion, country, progress, beauty, truth. What is wrong with these in the eyes of the young?

Religion.—The trouble here is partly intellectual, partly social. For intellectual reasons few able men have now the same intensity of religious belief as was possible for, say, St Thomas Aquinas. The God of most moderns is a little vague, and apt to degenerate into a Life Force or a 'power not ourselves that makes for righteousness'. Even believers are concerned much more with the effects of religion in this world than with that other world that they profess to believe in; they are not nearly so sure that this world was created for the glory of God as they are that God is a useful hypothesis for improving this world. By subordinating God to the needs of this sublunary life, they cast suspicion upon the genuinness of their faith. They seem to think that God, like the Sabbath, was made for man. There are also sociological reasons for not accepting the Churches as the basis of a modern idealism. The Churches, through their endowments, have become bound up with the defence of property. Moreover, they are connected with an oppressive ethic, which condemns many pleasures that to the young appear harmless and inflicts many torments that to the sceptical appear unnecessarily cruel. I have known earnest young men who accepted wholeheartedly the teaching of Christ; they found themselves in opposition to official Christianity, outcasts and victims of persecution, quite as much as if they had been militant atheists.

Country.—Patriotism has been in many times and places a passionate belief to which the best minds could give full assent. It was so in England in the time of Shakespeare, in Germany in the time of Fichte, in Italy in the time of Mazzini. It is so still in Poland, China, and Outer Mongolia. In the Western nations it is still immensely powerful: it controls politics, public expenditure, military preparations, and so on. But the intelligent youth are unable to accept it as an adequate ideal; they perceive that it is all very well for oppressed nations, but that as soon as an oppressed nation achieves its freedom, the nationalism which was formerly heroic becomes oppressive. The Poles, who had the sympathy of idealists ever since Maria Teresa 'wept but took', have used their freedom to organise oppression in Ukrania. The Irish, upon whom the British had inflicted civilisation for eight hundred years, have used their freedom to pass laws preventing the publication of many good books. The spectacle of the Poles murdering Ukrainians and the Irish murdering literature makes nationalism seem a somewhat inadequate ideal even for a small nation. But when it comes to a powerful nation, the argument is even stronger. The Treaty of Versailles was not very encouraging to those who had had the luck not to be killed in defending the ideals which their rulers betrayed. Those who during the war averred that they were combating militarism became at its conclusion the leading militarists in their respective countries. Such facts have made it obvious to all intelligent young men that patriotism is the chief curse of our age and will bring civilisation to an end if it cannot be mitigated.

Progress.—This is a nineteenth-century ideal which has too much Babbit about it for the sophisticated youth. Measurable progress is necessarily in unimportant things, such as the number of motor-cars made, or the number of peanuts consumed. The really important things are not measurable and are therefore not suitable for the methods of the booster. Moreover, many modern inventions tend to make people silly. I might instance the radio, the talkies, and poison gas. Shakespeare measured the excellence of an age by its style in poetry (see Sonnet XXXII), but this mode of measurement is out of date.

Beauty.—There is something that sounds old-fashioned about beauty, though it is hard to say why. A modern painter would be indignant if he were accused of seeking beauty. Most artists nowadays appear to be inspired by some kind of rage against the world so that they wish rather to give significant pain than to afford serene satisfaction. Moreover many kinds of beauty require that a man should take himself more seriously than is possible for an intelligent modern. A prominent citizen of a small city State, such as Athens or Florence, could without difficulty feel himself important. The earth was the centre of the Universe, man was the purpose of creation, his own city showed man at his best, and he himself was among the best in his own city. In such circumstances Aeschylus or Dante could take his own joys or sorrows seriously. He could feel that the emotions of the individual matter, and that tragic occurrences deserve to be celebrated in immortal verse. But the modern man, when misfortune assails him, is conscious of himself as a unit in a statistical total; the past and the future stretch before him in a dreary procession of trivial defeats. Man himself appears as a somewhat ridiculous strutting animal, shouting and fussing during a brief interlude between infinite silences.

'Unaccommodated man is no more but such a poor, bare, forked animal,' says King Lear, and the idea drives him to madness because it is unfamiliar. But to the modern man the idea is familiar and drives him only to triviality.

Truth.—In old days truth was absolute, eternal and super-human. Myself when young accepted this view and devoted a misspent youth to the search for truth. But a whole host of enemies have arisen to slay truth: pragmatism, behaviourism, psychologism, relativity-physics. Galileo and the Inquisition disagreed as to whether the earth went round the sun or the sun went round the earth. Both agreed in thinking that there was a great difference between these two opinions. The point on which they agreed was the one on which they were both mistaken: the difference is only one of words. In old days it was possible to worship truth; indeed the sincerity of the worship was demonstrated by the practice of human sacrifice. But it is difficult to worship a merely human and relative truth. The law of gravitation, according to Eddington, is only a convenient convention of measurement. It is not truer than other views, any more than the metric system is truer than feet and yards.

> Nature and Nature's law lay hid in night;
> God said, 'Let Newton be,' and measurement was facilitated.

This sentiment seems lacking in sublimity. When Spinoza believed anything, he considered that he was enjoying the intellectual love of God. The modern man believes either with Marx that he is swayed by economic motives, or with Freud that some sexual motive underlies his belief in the exponential theorem or in the distribution of fauna in the Red Sea. In neither case can he enjoy Spinoza's exaltation.

So far we have been considering modern cynicism in a rationalistic manner, as something that has intellectual causes. Belief, however, as modern psychologists are never weary of telling us, is seldom determined by rational motives, and the same is true of disbelief, though sceptics often overlook this fact. The causes of any widespread scepticism are likely to be sociological rather than intellectual. The main cause always is comfort without power. The holders of power are not cynical, since they are able to enforce their ideas. Victims of oppression are not cynical, since they are filled with hate, and hate, like any other strong passion, brings with it a train of attendant beliefs. Until the advent of education, democracy, and mass production, intellectuals had everywhere a considerable influence upon the march of affairs, which was by no means diminished if their heads were cut off. The modern intellectual finds himself in a quite different situation. It is by no means difficult for him to obtain a fat job and a good income provided he is willing to sell his services to the stupid rich either as propagandist or as Court jester. The effect of mass production and elementary education is that stupidity is more firmly entrenched than at any other time since the rise of civilisation. When the Czarist Government killed Lenin's brother, it did not turn Lenin into a cynic, since hatred inspired a lifelong activity in which he was finally successful. But in the more solid countries of the West there is seldom such potent cause for hatred, or such opportunity of spectacular revenge. The work of the intellectuals is ordered and paid for by Governments or rich men, whose aims probably seem absurd, if not pernicious, to the intellectuals concerned. But a dash of cynicism enables them to adjust their consciences to the situation. There are, it is true, some activities in which wholly admirable work is desired by the powers that be; the chief of these is science, and the next is public architecture in America. But if a man's education has been literary, as is still too often the case, he finds himself at the age of twenty-two with a considerable skill that he cannot exercise in any manner that appears important to himself. Men of science are not cynical even in the West, because they can exercise their best brains with the full approval of the community; but in this they are exceptionally fortunate among modern intellectuals.

If this diagnosis is right, modern cynicism cannot be cured merely by preaching, or by putting better ideals before the young than those that their pastors and masters fish out from the rusty armoury of outworn superstitions. The cure will only come when intellectuals can find a career that embodies their creative impulses. I do not see any prescription except the old one advocated by Disraeli: 'Educate our masters.' But it will have to be a more real education than is commonly given at the present day to either proletarians or plutocrats, and it will have to be an education taking some account of real cultural values and not only of the utilitarian desire to produce so many goods that nobody has time to enjoy them. A man is not allowed to practise medicine unless he knows something of the human body, but a financier is allowed to operate freely without any knowledge at all of the multifarious effects of his activities, with the sole exception of the effect upon his bank account. How pleasant a world would be in which no man was allowed to operate on the Stock Exchange unless he could pass an examination in economics and Greek poetry, and in which politicians were obliged to have a competent knowledge of history and modern novels! Imagine a magnate confronted with the question: 'If you were to make a corner in wheat, what effect would this have upon German poetry?' Causation in the modern world is more complex and remote in its ramifications than it ever was before, owing to the increase of large organisations; but those who control these organisations are ignorant men who do not know the hundredth part of the consequences of their actions. Rabelais published his book anonymously for fear of losing his University post. A modern Rabelais would never write the book, because he would be aware that his anonymity would be penetrated by the perfected methods of publicity. The rulers of the world have always been stupid, but have not in the past been so powerful as they are now. It is therefore more important than it used to be to find some way of securing that they shall be intelligent. Is this problem insoluble? I do not think so, but I should be the last to maintain that it is easy.

10

MODERN HOMOGENEITY[1]

The European traveller in America—at least if I may judge by myself—is struck by two peculiarities: first the extreme similarity of outlook in all parts of the United States (except the old South), and secondly the passionate desire of each locality to prove that it is peculiar and different from every other. The second of these is of course, caused by the first. Every place wishes to have a reason for local pride, and therefore cherishes whatever is distinctive in the way of geography or history or tradition. The greater the uniformity that in fact exists, the more eager becomes the search for differences that may mitigate it. The old South is in fact quite unlike the rest of America, so unlike that one feels as if one had arrived in a different country. It is agricultural, aristocratic, and retrospective, whereas the rest of America is industrial, democratic and prospective. When I say that America outside the old South is industrial, I am thinking even of those parts that are devoted almost wholly to agriculture,

[1] Written in 1930.

for the mentality of the American agriculturist is industrial. He uses much modern machinery; he is intimately dependent upon the railway and the telephone; he is very conscious of the distant markets to which his products are sent; he is in fact a capitalist who might just as well be in some other business. A peasant, as he exists in Europe and Asia, is practically unknown in the United States. This is an immense boon to America, and perhaps its most important superiority as compared to the Old World, for the peasant everywhere is cruel, avaricious, conservative, and inefficient. I have seen orange groves in Sicily and orange groves in California; the contrast represents a period of about two thousand years. Orange groves in Sicily are remote from trains and ships; the trees are old and gnarled and beautiful; the methods are those of classical antiquity. The men are ignorant and semi-savage, mongrel descendants of Roman slaves and Arab invaders; what they lack in intelligence towards trees they make up for by cruelty to animals. With moral degradation and economic incompetence goes an instinctive sense of beauty which is perpetually reminding one of Theocritus and the myth about the Garden of the Hesperides. In a Californian orange grove the Garden of the Hesperides seems very remote. The trees are all exactly alike, carefully tended and at the right distance apart. The oranges, it is true, are not all exactly of the same size, but careful machinery sorts them so that automatically all those in one box are exactly similar. They travel along with suitable things being done to them by suitable machines at suitable points until they enter a suitable refrigerator car in which they travel to a suitable market. The machine stamps the word 'Sunkist' upon them, but otherwise there is nothing to suggest that nature has any part in their production. Even the climate is artificial, for when there would otherwise be frost, the orange grove is kept artificially warm by a pall of smoke. The men engaged in agriculture of this kind do not feel themselves, like the agriculturists of former times, the patient servants of natural forces; on the contrary, they feel themselves the masters, and able to bend natural forces to their will. There is therefore not the same difference in America as in the Old World between the outlook of industrialists and that of agriculturists. The important part of the environment in America is the human part; by comparison the non-human part sinks into insignificance. I was constantly assured in Southern California that the climate turned people into lotus eaters, but I confess I saw no evidence of this. They seemed to me exactly like the people in Minneapolis or Winnipeg, although climate, scenery, and natural conditions were as different as possible in the two regions. When one considers the difference between a Norwegian and a Sicilian, and compares it with the lack of difference between a man from (say) North Dakota and a man from Southern California, one realises the immense revolution in human affairs which has been brought about by man's becoming the master instead of the slave of his physical environment. Norway and Sicily both have ancient traditions; they had pre-Christian religions embodying men's reactions to the climate, and when Christianity came it inevitably took very different forms in the two countries. The Norwegian feared ice and snow; the Sicilian feared lava and earthquakes. Hell was invented in a southern climate; if it had been invented in Norway, it would have been cold. But neither in North Dakota nor in Southern California is Hell a climatic condition: in both it is a stringency on the money market. This illustrates the unimportance of climate in modern life.

America is a man-made world; moreover it is a world which man has made by means of machinery. I am thinking not only of the physical environment, but also and quite as much of thoughts and emotions. Consider a really stirring murder: the murderer, it is true, may be primitive in his methods, but those who spread the knowledge of his deed do so by means of all the latest resources of science. Not only in the great cities, but in lonely farms on the prairie and in mining camps in the Rockies, the radio disseminates all the latest information, so that half the topics of conversation on a given day are the same in every household throughout the country. As I was crossing the plains in the train, endeavouring not to hear a loud-speaker bellowing advertisements of soap, an old farmer came up to me with a beaming face and said, 'Wherever you go nowadays you can't get away from civilisation.' Alas! How true! I was endeavouring to read Virginia Woolf, but the advertisements won the day.

Uniformity in the physical apparatus of life would be no grave matter, but uniformity in matters of thought and opinion is much more dangerous. It is, however, a quite inevitable result of modern inventions. Production is cheaper when it is unified and on a large scale than when it is divided into a number of small units. This applies quite as much to the production of opinions as to the production of pins. The principal sources of opinion in the present day are the schools, the Churches, the Press, the cinema, and the radio. The teaching in the elementary schools must inevitably become more and more standardised as more use is made of apparatus. It may, I think, be assumed that both the cinema and the radio will play a rapidly increasing part in school education in the near future. This will mean that the lessons will be produced at a centre and will be precisely the same wherever the material prepared at this centre is used. Some Churches, I am told, send out every week a model sermon to all the less educated of their clergy, who, if they are governed by the ordinary laws of human nature, are no doubt grateful for being saved the trouble of composing a sermon of their own. This model sermon, of course, deals with some burning topic of the moment, and aims at arousing a given mass emotion throughout the length and breadth of the land. The same thing applies in a higher degree to the Press, which receives everywhere the same telegraphic news and is syndicated on a large scale. Reviews of my books, I find, are, except in the best newspapers, verbally the same from New York to San Francisco, and from Maine to Texas, except that they become shorter as one travels from the north-east to the south-west.

Perhaps the greatest of all forces for uniformity in the modern world is the cinema, since its influence is not confined to America but penetrates to all parts of the world, except the Soviet Union, which, however, has its own different uniformity. The cinema embodies, broadly speaking, Hollywood's opinion of what is liked in the Middle West. Our emotions in regard to love and marriage, birth and death are becoming standardised according to this recipe. To the young of all lands Hollywood represents the last word in modernity, displaying both the pleasures of the rich and the methods to be adopted for acquiring riches. I suppose the talkies will lead before long to the adoption of a universal language, which will be that of Hollywood.

It is not only among the comparatively ignorant that there is uniformity in America. The same thing applies, though in a slightly less degree, to culture. I visited book shops in every part of the country, and found everywhere the same best-sellers prominently displayed. So far as I could judge, the cultured ladies of America buy every year about a dozen books, the same dozen everywhere. To an author this is a very satisfactory state of affairs, provided he is one of the dozen. But it certainly does mark a difference from Europe, where there are many books with small sales rather than a few with large sales.

It must not be supposed that the tendency towards uniformity is either wholly good or wholly bad. It has great advantages and also great disadvantages: its chief advantage is, of course, that it produces a population capable of peaceable co-operation; its great disadvantage is that it produces a population prone to per-secution of minorities. This latter defect is probably temporary, since it may be assumed that before long there will be no minor-ities. A great deal depends, of course, on how the uniformity is achieved. Take, for example, what the schools do to southern Italians. Southern Italians have been distinguished throughout history for murder, graft, and aesthetic sensibility. The Public Schools effectively cure them of the last of these three, and to that extent assimilate them to the native American population, but in regard to the other two distinctive qualities, I gather that the success of the schools is less marked. This illustrates one of the dangers of uniformity as an aim: good qualities are easier to destroy than bad ones, and therefore uniformity is most easily achieved by lowering all standards. It is, of course, clear that a country with a large foreign population must endeavour, through its schools, to assimilate the children of immigrants, and therefore a certain degree of Americanisation is inevitable. It is, however, unfortunate that such a large part of this process should be effected by means of a somewhat blatant nationalism. America is already the strongest country in the world, and its preponderance is continually increasing. This fact naturally inspires fear in Europe, and the fear is increased by everything suggesting militant nationalism. It may be the destiny of America to teach political good sense to Europe, but I am afraid that the pupil is sure to prove refractory.

With the tendency towards uniformity in America there goes, as it seems to me, a mistaken conception of democracy. It seems to be generally held in the United States that democracy requires all men to be alike, and that, if a man is in any way different from another, he is 'setting himself up' as superior to that other. France is quite as democratic as America, and yet this idea does not exist in France. The doctor, the lawyer, the priest, the public official are all different types in France; each profession has its own traditions and its own standards, although it does not set up to be superior to other professions. In America all professional men are assimilated in type to the business man. It is as though one should decree that an orchestra should consist only of violins. There does not seem to be an adequate understanding of the fact that society should be a pattern or an organism, in which different organs play different parts. Imagine the eye and the ear quarrelling as to whether it is better to see or to hear, and deciding that each would do neither since neither could do both. This, it seems to me, would be democracy as understood in America. There is a strange envy of any kind of excellence which cannot be universal, except, of course, in the sphere of athletics and sport, where aristocracy is enthusiastically acclaimed. It seems that the average American is more capable of humility in regard to his muscles than in regard to his brains; perhaps this is because his admiration for muscle is more profound and genuine than his admiration of brains. The flood of popular scientific books in America is inspired partly, though of course not wholly, by the unwillingness to admit that there is anything in science which only experts can understand. The idea that a special training may be necessary to understand, say, the theory of relativity, causes a sort of irritation, although nobody is irritated by the fact that a special training is necessary in order to be a first-rate football player.

Achieved eminence is perhaps more admired in America than in any other country, and yet the road to certain kinds of eminence is made very difficult for the young, because people are intolerant of any eccentricity or anything that could be called 'setting one's self up', provided the person concerned is not already labelled 'eminent'. Consequently many of the finished types that are most admired are difficult to produce at home and have to be imported from Europe. This fact is bound up with standardisation and uniformity. Exceptional merit, especially in artistic directions, is bound to meet with great obstacles in youth so long as everybody is expected to conform outwardly to a pattern set by the successful executive.

Standardisation, though it may have disadvantages for the exceptional individual, probably increases the happiness of the average man, since he can utter his thoughts with a certainty that they will be thoughts of his hearer. Moreover it promotes national cohesion, and makes politics less bitter and violent than where more marked differences exist. I do not think it is possible to strike a balance of gains and losses, but I think the standardisation which now exists in America is likely to exist throughout Europe as the world becomes more mechanised. Europeans, therefore, who find fault with America on this account should realise that they are finding fault with the future of their own countries, and are setting themselves against an inevitable and universal trend in civilisation. Undoubtedly internationalism will become easier as the differences between nations diminish, and if once internationalism were established, social cohesion would become of enormous importance for preserving internal peace. There is a certain risk, which cannot be denied, of an immobility analogous to that of the late Roman Empire. But as against this, we may set the revolutionary forces of modern science and modern technique. Short of a universal intellectual decay, these forces, which are a new feature in the modern world, will make immobility impossible, and prevent that kind of stagnation which has overtaken great empires in the past. Arguments from history are dangerous to apply to the present and the future, because of the complete change that science has introduced. I see therefore no reason for undue pessimism, however standardisation may offend the tastes of those who are unaccustomed to it.

11

MEN *VERSUS* INSECTS[1]

Amid wars and rumours of wars, while 'disarmament' proposals and non-aggression pacts threaten the human race with unprecedented disaster, another conflict, perhaps even more important, is receiving much less notice than it deserves—I mean the conflict between men and insects.

We are accustomed to being the Lords of Creation; we no longer have occasion, like the cave men, to fear lions and tigers, mammoths and wild boars. Except against each other, we feel ourselves safe. But while big animals no longer threaten our existence, it is otherwise with small animals. Once before in the history of life on this planet, large animals gave place to small ones. For many ages dinosaurs ranged unconcerned through swamp and forest, fearing nothing but each other, not doubting the absoluteness of their empire. But they disappeared, to give place to tiny mammals—mice, small hedgehogs, miniature horses no bigger than rats, and such-like. Why the dinosaurs

[1] Written in 1933.

died out is not known, but it is supposed to be that they had minute brains and devoted themselves to the growth of weapons of offence in the shape of numerous horns. However that may be, it was not through their line that life developed.

The mammals, having become supreme, proceeded to grow big. But the biggest on land, the mammoth, is extinct, and the other large animals have grown rare, except man and those that he has domesticated. Man, by his intelligence, has succeeded in finding nourishing for a large population, in spite of his size. He is safe, except from the little creatures—the insects and the micro-organisms.

Insects have an initial advantage in their numbers. A small wood may easily contain as many ants as there are human beings in the whole world. They have another advantage in the fact that they eat our food before it is ripe for us. Many noxious insects which used to live only in some one comparatively small region have been unintentionally transported by man to new environments where they have done immense damage. Travel and trade are useful to insects as well as to micro-organisms. Yellow fever formerly existed only in West Africa, but was carried to the Western hemisphere by the slave trade. Now, owing to the opening up of Africa, it is gradually travelling eastward across that continent. When it reaches the east coast it will become almost impossible to keep it out of India and China, where it may be expected to halve the population. Sleeping sickness is an even more deadly African disease which is gradually spreading.

Fortunately science has discovered ways by which insect pests can be kept under. Most of them are liable to parasites which kill so many that the survivors cease to be a serious problem, and entomologists are engaged in studying and breeding such parasites. Official reports of their activities are fascinating; they are full of such sentences as: 'He proceeded to Brazil, at the request of the planters of Trinidad, to search for the natural enemies of the sugar-cane Froghopper.' One would say that the sugar-cane

Froghopper would have little chance in this context. Unfortunately, so long as war continues, all scientific knowledge is double-edged. For example, Professor Fritz Haber, who has just died, invented a process for the fixation of nitrogen. He intended it to increase the fertility of the soil, but the German Government used if for the manufacture of high explosives, and has recently exiled him for preferring manure to bombs. In the next great war, the scientists on either side will let loose pests on the crops of the other side, and it may prove scarcely possible to destroy the pests when peace comes. The more we know, the more harm we can do each other. If human beings in their rage against each other, invoke the aid of insects and micro-organisms, as they certainly will do if there is another big war, it is by no means unlikely that the insects will remain the sole ultimate victors. Perhaps, from a cosmic point of view, this is not to be regretted; but as a human being I cannot help heaving a sigh over my own species.

12

EDUCATION AND DISCIPLINE

Any serious educational theory must consist of two parts: a conception of the ends of life, and a science of psychological dynamics, i.e. of the laws of mental change. Two men who differ as to the ends of life cannot hope to agree about education. The educational machine, throughout Western civilisation, is dominated by two ethical theories: that of Christianity, and that of nationalism. These two, when taken seriously, are incompatible, as is becoming evident in Germany, For my part, I hold that, where they differ, Christianity is preferable, but where they agree, both are mistaken. The conception which I should substitute as the purpose of education is civilisation, a term which, as I mean it, has a definition which is partly individual, partly social. It consists, in the individual, of both intellectual and moral qualities: intellectually, a certain minimum of general knowledge, technical skill in one's own profession, and a habit of forming opinions on evidence; morally, of impartiality, kindliness, and a modicum of self-control. I should add a quality which is neither moral nor intellectual, but perhaps physiological: zest and joy of life. In communities, civilisation demands respect for law, justice as between man and man, purposes not involving permanent injury to any section of the human race, and intelligent adaptation of means to ends.

If these are to be the purpose of education, it is a question for the science of psychology to consider what can be done towards realising them, and, in particular, what degree of freedom is likely to prove most effective.

On the question of freedom in education there are at present three main schools of thought, deriving partly from differences as to ends and partly from differences in psychological theory. There are those who say that children should be completely free, however bad they may be; there are those who say they should be completely subject to authority, however good they may be; and there are those who say they should be free, but in spite of freedom they should be always good. This last party is larger than it has any logical right to be; children, like adults, will not all be virtuous if they are all free. The belief that liberty will ensure moral perfection is a relic of Rousseauism, and would not survive a study of animals and babies. Those who hold this belief think that education should have no positive purpose, but should merely offer an environment suitable for spontaneous development. I cannot agree with this school, which seems to me too individualistic, and unduly indifferent to the importance of knowledge. We live in communities which require co-operation, and it would be utopian to expect all the necessary co-operation to result from spontaneous impulse. The existence of a large population on a limited area is only possible owing to science and technique; education must, therefore, hand on the necessary minimum of these. The educators who allow most freedom are men whose success depends upon a degree of benevolence, self-control, and trained intelligence which can hardly be generated where every impulse is left unchecked; their merits, therefore, are not likely to be perpetuated if their methods are undiluted.

Education, viewed from a social standpoint, must be something more positive than a mere opportunity for growth. It must, of course, provide this, but it must also provide a mental and moral equipment which children cannot acquire entirely for themselves.

The arguments in favour of a great degree of freedom in education are derived not from man's natural goodness, but from the effects of authority, both on those who suffer it and on those who exercise it. Those who are subject to authority become either submissive or rebellious, and each attitude has its drawbacks.

The submissive lose initiative, both in thought and action; moreover, the anger generated by the feeling of being thwarted tends to find an outlet in bullying those who are weaker. That is why tyrannical institutions are self-perpetuating: what a man has suffered from his father he inflicts upon his son, and the humiliations which he remembers having endured at his public school he passes on to 'natives' when he becomes an empire-builder. Thus an unduly authoritative education turns the pupils into timid tyrants, incapable of either claiming or tolerating originality in word or deed. The effect upon the educators is even worse: they tend to become sadistic disciplinarians, glad to inspire terror, and content to inspire nothing else. As these men represent knowledge, the pupils acquire a horror of knowledge, which, among the English upper-class, is supposed to be part of human nature, but is really part of the well-grounded hatred of the authoritarian pedagogue.

Rebels, on the other hand, though they may be necessary, can hardly be just to what exists. Moreover, there are many ways of rebelling, and only a small minority of these are wise. Galileo was a rebel and was wise; believers in the flat-earth theory are equally rebels, but are foolish. There is a great danger in the tendency to suppose that opposition to authority is essentially meritorious and that unconventional opinions are bound to be correct: no useful purpose is served by smashing lamp-posts or maintaining Shakespeare to be no poet. Yet this excessive rebelliousness is often the effect that too much authority has on spirited pupils. And when rebels become educators, they sometimes encourage defiance in their pupils, for whom at the same time they are trying to produce a perfect environment, although these two aims are scarcely compatible.

What is wanted is neither submissiveness nor rebellion, but good nature, and general friendliness both to people and to new ideas. These qualities are due in part to physical causes, to which old-fashioned educators paid too little attention; but they are due still more to freedom from the feeling of baffled impotence which arises when vital impulses are thwarted. If the young are to grow into friendly adults, it is necessary, in most cases, that they should feel their environment friendly. This requires that there should be a certain sympathy with the child's important desires, and not merely an attempt to use him for some abstract end such as the glory of God or the greatness of one's country. And, in teaching, every attempt should be made to cause the pupil to feel that it is worth his while to know what is being taught—at least when this is true. When the pupil co-operates willingly, he learns twice as fast and with half the fatigue. All these are valid reasons for a very great degree of freedom.

It is easy, however, to carry the argument too far. It is not desirable that children, in avoiding the vices of the slave, should acquire those of the aristocrat. Consideration for others, not only in great matters, but also in little everyday things, is an essential element in civilisation, without which social life would be intolerable. I am not thinking of mere forms of politeness, such as saying 'please' and 'thank you': formal manners are most fully developed among barbarians, and diminish with every advance in culture. I am thinking rather of willingness to take a fair share of necessary work, to be obliging in small ways that save trouble on the balance. Sanity itself is a form of politeness and it is not desirable to give a child a sense of omnipotence, or a belief that adults exist only to minister to the pleasures of the young. And those who disapprove of the existence of the idle rich are hardly consistent if they bring up their children without any sense that work is necessary, and without the habits that make continuous application possible.

There is another consideration to which some advocates of freedom attach too little importance. In a community of children which is left without adult interference there is a tyranny of the stronger, which is likely to be far more brutal than most adult tyranny. If two children of two or three years old are left to play together, they will, after a few fights, discover which is bound to be the victor, and the other will then become a slave. Where the number of children is larger, one or two acquire complete mastery, and the others have far less liberty than they would have if the adults interfered to protect the weaker and less pugnacious. Consideration for others does not, with most children, arise spontaneously, but has to be taught, and can hardly be taught except by the exercise of authority. This is perhaps the most important argument against the abdication of the adults.

I do not think that educators have yet solved the problem of combining the desirable forms of freedom with the necessary minimum of moral training. The right solution, it must be admitted, is often made impossible by parents before the child is brought to an enlightened school. Just as psychoanalysts, from their clinical experience, conclude that we are all mad, so the authorities in modern schools, from their contact with pupils whose parents have made them unmanageable, are disposed to conclude all children are 'difficult' and all parents utterly foolish. Children who have been driven wild by parental tyranny (which often takes the form of solicitous affection) may require a longer or shorter period of complete liberty before they can view any adult without suspicion. But children who have been sensibly handled at home can bear to be checked in minor ways, so long as they feel that they are being helped in the ways that they them-selves regard as important. Adults who like children, and are not reduced to a condition of nervous exhaustion by their company, can achieve a great deal in the way of discipline without ceasing to be regarded with friendly feelings by their pupils.

I think modern educational theorists are inclined to attach too much importance to the negative virtue of not interfering with children, and too little to the positive merit of enjoying their company. If you have the sort of liking for children that many people have for horses or dogs, they will be apt to respond to your suggestions, and to accept prohibitions, perhaps with some good-humoured grumbling, but without resentment. It is no use to have the sort of liking that consists in regarding them as a field for valuable social endeavour, or—what amounts to the same thing—as an outlet for power-impulses. No child will be grateful for an interest in him that springs from the thought that he will have a vote to be secured for your party or a body to be sacrificed to king and country. The desirable sort of interest is that which consists in spontaneous pleasure in the presence of children, without any ulterior purpose. Teachers who have this quality will seldom need to interfere with children's freedom, but will be able to do so, when necessary, without causing psychological damage.

Unfortunately, it is utterly impossible for overworked teachers to preserve an instinctive liking for children; they are bound to come to feel towards them as the proverbial confectioner's apprentice does towards macaroons. I do not think that educa-tion ought to be anyone's whole profession: it should be under-taken for at most two hours a day by people whose remaining hours are spent away from children. The society of the young is fatiguing, especially when strict discipline is avoided. Fatigue, in the end, produces irritation, which is likely to express itself somehow, whatever theories the harassed teacher may have taught himself or herself to believe. The necessary friendliness cannot be preserved by self-control alone. But where it exists, it should be unnecessary to have rules in advance as to how 'naughty' children are to be treated, since impulse is likely to lead to the right decision, and almost any decision will be right if the child feels that you like him. No rules, however wise, are a substitute for affection and tact.

13

STOICISM AND MENTAL HEALTH[1]

By means of modern psychology, many educational problems which were formerly tackled (very unsuccessfully) by sheer moral discipline are now solved by more indirect but also more scientific methods. There is, perhaps, a tendency, especially among the less well-informed devotees of psychoanalysis, to think that there is no longer any need of stoic self-command. I do not hold this view, and in the present essay I wish to consider some of the situations which make it necessary, and some of the methods by which it can be created in young people; also some of the dangers to be avoided in creating it.

Let us begin at once with the most difficult and most essential of the problems that call for stoicism: I mean, Death. There are various ways of attempting to cope with the fear of death. We may try to ignore it; we may never mention it, and always try to turn our thoughts in another direction when we find ourselves

[1] Written in 1928.

dwelling on it. This is the method of the butterfly people in Wells's *Time Machine*. Or we may adopt the exactly opposite course, and meditate continually concerning the brevity of human life, in the hope that familiarity will breed contempt; this was the course adopted by Charles V in his cloister after his abdication. There was a Fellow of a Cambridge College who even went so far as to sleep with his coffin in the room, and who used to go out on to the College lawns with a spade to cut worms in two, saying as he did so: 'Yah! you haven't got me yet.' There is a third course, which has been very widely adopted, and that is, to persuade oneself and others that death is not death, but the gateway to a new and better life. These three methods, mingled in varying proportions, cover most people's accommodations to the uncomfortable fact that we die.

To each of these methods, however, there are objections. The attempt to avoid thinking about an emotionally interesting subject, as the Freudians have pointed out in connection with sex, is sure to be unsuccessful, and to lead to various kinds of undesirable contortions. Now it may, of course, be possible, in the life of a child, to ward off knowledge of death, in any poignant form, throughout the earlier years. Whether this happens or not, is a matter of luck. If a parent or brother or sister dies, there is nothing to be done to prevent a child from acquiring an emotional awareness of death. Even if, by luck, the fact of death does not become vivid to a child in early years, it must do so sooner or later; and in those who are quite unprepared, there is likely to be a serious loss of balance when this occurs. We must therefore seek to establish some attitude towards death other than that of merely ignoring it.

The practice of brooding continually on death is at least equally harmful. It is a mistake to think too exclusively about any one subject, more particularly when our own thinking cannot issue in action. We can, of course, act so as to postpone our own death, and within limits every normal person does so. But we cannot prevent ourselves from dying ultimately; this is, therefore, a profitless subject of meditation. Moreover, it tends to diminish a man's interest in other people and events, and it is only objective interests that can preserve mental health. Fear of death makes a man feel himself the slave of external forces, and from a slave mentality no good result can follow. If, by meditation, a man could genuinely cure himself of the fear of death, he would cease to meditate on the subject; so long as it absorbs his thoughts, that proves that he has not ceased to fear it. This method, therefore, is no better than the other.

The belief that death is a gateway to a better life ought, logically, to prevent men from feeling any fear of death. Fortunately for the medical profession, it does not in fact have this effect, except in a few rare instances. One does not find that believers in a future life are less afraid of illness or more courageous in battle than those who think that death ends all. The late F. W. H. Myers used to tell how he asked a man at a dinner table what he thought would happen to him when he died. The man tried to ignore the question, but, on being pressed, replied: 'Oh, well, I suppose I shall inherit eternal bliss, but I wish you wouldn't talk about such unpleasant subjects.' The reason for this apparent inconsistency is, of course, that religious belief, in most people, exists only in the region of conscious thought, and has not succeeded in modifying unconscious mechanisms. If the fear of death is to be coped with successfully, it must be by some method which affects behaviour as a whole, not only that part of behaviour that is commonly called conscious thought. In a few instances, religious belief can effect this, but not in the majority of mankind. Apart from behaviouristic reasons, there are two other sources of this failure: one is a certain doubt which persists in spite of fervent professions, and shows itself in the form of anger with sceptics; the other is the fact that believers in a future life tend to emphasise, rather than minimise, the horror that would attach to death if their beliefs were unfounded, and so to increase fear in those who do not feel absolute certainty.

What, then, shall we do with young people to adapt them to a world in which death exists? We have to achieve three objects, which are very difficult to combine. (1) We must give them no feeling that death is a subject about which we do not wish to speak or to encourage them to think. If we give them such a feeling, they will conclude that there is an interesting mystery, and will think all the more. On this point, the familiar modern position on sex education is applicable. (2) We must nevertheless so act as to prevent them, if we can, from thinking much or often on the matter of death; there is the same kind of objection to such absorption as to absorption in pornography, namely that it diminishes efficiency, prevents all-round development, and leads to conduct which is unsatisfactory both to the person concerned and to others. (3) We must not hope to create in anyone a satisfactory attitude on the subject of death by means of conscious thought alone; more particularly, no good is done by beliefs intended to show that death is less terrible than it otherwise would be, when (as is usual) such beliefs do not penetrate below the level of consciousness.

To give effect to these various objects, we shall have to adopt somewhat different methods according to the experience of the child or young person. If no one closely connected with the child dies, it is fairly easy to secure an acceptance of death as a common fact, of no great emotional interest. So long as death is abstract and impersonal, it should be mentioned in a matter-of-fact voice, not as something terrible. If the child asks, 'Shall I die?' one should say, 'Yes, but probably not for a long time.' It is important to prevent any sense of mystery about death. It should be brought into the same category with the wearing out of toys. But it is certainly desirable, if possible, to make it seem very distant while children are young.

When someone of importance to the child dies, the matter is different. Suppose, for example, the child loses a brother. The parents are unhappy, and although they may not wish the child to know *how* unhappy they are, it is right and necessary that he should perceive *something* of what they suffer. Natural affection is of very great importance, and the child should feel that his elders feel it. Moreover, if, by superhuman efforts, they conceal their sorrow from the child, he may think: 'They wouldn't mind if I died.' Such a thought might start all kinds of morbid developments. Therefore, although the shock of such an occurrence is harmful when it occurs during late childhood (in early childhood it will not be felt much), yet, if it occurs, we must not minimise it too much. The subject must be neither avoided nor dwelt upon; what is possible, without any too obvious intention, must be done to create fresh interest, and above all fresh affections. I think that very intense affection for some one individual, in a child, is not infrequently a mark of something amiss. Such affection may arise towards one parent if the other parent is unkind, or towards a teacher if both parents are unkind. It is generally a product of fear: the object of affection is the only person who gives a sense of safety. Affection of this kind, in childhood, is not wholesome. Where it exists the death of the person loved may shatter the child's life. Even if all seems well outwardly, every subsequent love will be filled with terror. Husband (or wife) and children will be plagued by undue solicitude, and will be thought heartless when they are merely living their own lives. A parent ought not, therefore, to feel pleased at being the object of this kind of affection. If the child has a generally friendly environment and is happy, he will without much trouble get over the pain of any one loss that may happen to him. The impulse to life and hope ought to be sufficient, provided the normal opportunities for growth and happiness exist.

During adolescence, however, there is need of something more positive in the way of attitude towards death, if adult life is to be satisfactory. The adult should think little about death, either his own or that of people whom he loves, not because he deliberately turns his thoughts to other things, for that is a useless exercise which never really succeeds, but because of the multiplicity of his interests and activities. When he does think of death, it is best to think with a certain stoicism, deliberately and calmly, not attempting to minimise its importance, but feeling a certain pride in rising above it. The principle is the same as in the case of any other terror: resolute contemplation of the terrifying object is the only possible treatment. One must say to oneself: 'Well, yes, that might happen, but what of it?' People achieve this in such a case as death in battle, because they are then firmly persuaded of the importance of the cause to which they have given their life, or the life of someone dear to them. Something of this way of feeling is desirable at all times. At all times, a man should feel that there are matters of importance for which he lives, and that his death, or the death of wife or child, does not put an end to all that interests him in the world. If this attitude is to be genuine and profound in adult life, it is necessary that, in adolescence, a youth should be fired with generous enthusiasms, and that he should build his life and career about them. Adolescence is the period of generosity, and it should be utilised for the formation of generous habits. This can be achieved by the influence of the father or of the teacher. In a better community, the mother would often be the one to do it, but as a rule, at present, the lives of women are such as to make their outlook too personal and not sufficiently intellectual for what I have in mind. For the same reason, adolescents (female as well as male) ought, as a rule, to have men among their teachers, until a new generation of women has grown up which is more impersonal in its interests.

The place of stoicism in life has, perhaps, been somewhat underestimated in recent times, particularly by progressive educationists. When misfortune threatens, there are two ways of dealing with the situation: we may try to avoid the misfortune, or we may decide that we will meet it with fortitude. The former method is admirable where it is available without cowardice; but the latter is necessary, sooner or later, for anyone who is not prepared to be the slave of fear. This attitude constitutes stoicism. The great difficulty, for an educator, is that the instilling of stoicism in the young affords an outlet for sadism. In the past, ideas of discipline were so fierce that education became a channel for impulses of cruelty. Is it possible to give the necessary minimum of discipline without developing a pleasure in making the child suffer? Old-fashioned people will, of course, deny that they feel any such pleasure. Everyone knows the story of the boy whose father, while administering the cane, said: 'My boy, this hurts me more than it does you'; to which the boy replied: 'Then, father, will you let me do it to you instead?' Samuel Butler, in *The Way of all Flesh*, has depicted the sadistic pleasures of stern parents in a way which is convincing to any student of modern psychology. What, then, are we to do about it?

The fear of death is only one of many that are best dealt with by stoicism. There is the fear of poverty, the fear of physical pain, the fear of childbirth which is common among well-to-do women. All such fears are weakening and more or less contemptible. But if we take the line that people ought not to mind such things, we shall tend also to take the line that nothing need be done to mitigate evils. For a long time, it was thought that women ought not to have anaesthetics in childbirth; in Japan, this opinion persists to the present day. Male doctors held that anaesthetics would be harmful; there was no reason for this view, which was doubtless due to unconscious sadism. But the more the pains of childbirth have been mitigated, the less willing rich women have become to endure them: their courage has diminished faster than the need of it. Evidently there must be a balance. It is impossible to make the whole of life soft and pleasant, and therefore human beings must be capable of an attitude suitable to the unpleasant portions; but we must try to bring this about with as little encouragement to cruelty as possible.

Whoever has to deal with young children soon learns that too much sympathy is a mistake. Too little sympathy is, of course, a worse mistake, but in this, as in everything else, each extreme is bad. A child that invariably receives sympathy will continue to cry over every tiny mishap; the ordinary self-control of the average adult is only achieved through knowledge that no sympathy will be won by making a fuss. Children readily understand that an adult who is sometimes a little stern is best for them; their instinct tells them whether they are loved or not, and from those whom they feel to be affectionate they will put up with whatever strictness results from genuine desire for their proper development. Thus in theory the solution is simple: let educators be inspired by wise love, and they will do the right thing. In fact, however, the matter is more complicated. Fatigue, vexation, worry, impatience, beset the parent or teacher, and it is dangerous to have an educational theory which allows the adult to vent these feelings upon the child for the sake of his ultimate welfare. Nevertheless, if the theory is true, it must be accepted, and the dangers must be brought before the consciousness of the parent or teacher, so that everything possible may be done to guard against them.

We can now sum up the conclusions suggested by the foregoing discussion. In regard to the painful hazards of life, knowledge of them, on the part of children, should be neither avoided nor obtruded; it should come when circumstances make it unavoidable. Painful things, when they have to be mentioned, should be treated truthfully and unemotionally, except when a death occurs in the family, in which case it would be unnatural to conceal sorrow. The adults should display in their own conduct a certain gay courage, which the young will unconsciously acquire from their example. In adolescence, large impersonal interests should be set before the young, and education should be so conducted as to give them the idea (by suggestion, not by explicit exhortation) of living for purposes outside themselves.

They should be taught to endure misfortune, when it comes, by remembering that there are still things to live for; but they should not brood on possible misfortunes, even for the purpose of being prepared to meet them. Those whose business it is to deal with the young must keep a close watch upon themselves to see that they do not derive a sadistic pleasure from the necessary element of discipline in education; the motive for discipline must always be the development of character or intelligence. For the intellect, also, requires discipline, without which accuracy will never be achieved. But the discipline of the intellect is a different topic, and lies outside the scope of this essay.

I have only one more word to say, and that is, that discipline is best when it springs from an inner impulse. In order that this may be possible, it is necessary that the child or adolescent should feel the ambition to achieve something difficult, and should be willing to make efforts to that end. Such ambition is usually suggested by some person in the environment; thus even self-discipline depends, in the end, upon an educational stimulus.

14

ON COMETS

If I were a comet, I should consider the men of our present age a degenerate breed.

In former times, the respect for comets was universal and profound. One of them foreshadowed the death of Caesar; another was regarded as indicating the approaching death of the Emperor Vespasian. He himself was a strong-minded man, and maintained that the comet must have some other significance, since it was hairy and he was bald; but there were few who shared this extreme of rationalism. The Venerable Bede said that 'comets portend revolutions of kingdoms, pestilence, war, winds, or heat'. John Knox regarded comets as evidences of divine anger, and other Scottish Protestants thought them 'a warning to the King to extirpate the Papists'.

America, and especially New England, came in for a due share of cometary attention. In 1652 a comet appeared just at the moment when the eminent Mr Cotton fell ill, and disappeared at his death. Only ten years later, the wicked inhabitants of Boston were warned by a new comet to abstain from 'voluptuousness and abuse of the good creatures of God by licentiousness in drinking and fashions in apparel'. Increase Mather, the eminent divine, considered that comets and eclipses had portended the deaths of Presidents of Harvard and Colonial Governors, and instructed his flock to pray to the Lord that he would not 'take away stars and send comets to succeed them'.

All this superstition was gradually dispelled by Halley's discovery that one comet, at least, went round the sun in an orderly ellipse, just like a sensible planet, and by Newton's proof that comets obey the law of gravitation. For some time, Professors in the more old-fashioned universities were forbidden to mention these discoveries, but in the long run the truth could not be concealed.

In our day, it is difficult to imagine a world in which everybody, high and low, educated and uneducated, was preoccupied with comets, and filled with terror whenever one appeared. Most of us have never seen a comet. I have seen two, but they were far less impressive than I had expected them to be. The cause of the change in our attitude is not merely rationalism, but artificial lighting. In the streets of a modern city the night sky is invisible; in rural districts, we move in cars with bright headlights. We have blotted out the heavens, and only a few scientists remain aware of stars and planets, meteorites and comets. The world of our daily life is more man-made than at any previous epoch. In this there is loss as well as gain: Man, in the security of his dominion, is becoming trivial, arrogant, and a little mad. But I do not think a comet would now produce the wholesome moral effect which it produced in Boston in 1662; a stronger medicine would now be needed.

15

WHAT IS THE SOUL?[1]

One of the most painful circumstances of recent advances in science is that each one of them makes us know less than we thought we did. When I was young we all knew, or thought we knew, that a man consists of a soul and a body; that the body is in time and space, but the soul is in time only. Whether the soul survives death was a matter as to which opinions might differ, but that there is a soul was thought to be indubitable. As for the body, the plain man of course considered its existence self-evident, and so did the man of science, but the philosopher was apt to analyse it away after one fashion or another, reducing it usually to ideas in the mind of the man who had the body and anybody else who happened to notice him. The philosopher, however, was not taken seriously, and science remained comfortably materialistic, even in the hands of quite orthodox scientists.

Nowadays these fine old simplicities are lost: physicists assure as that there is no such thing as matter, and psychologists assure

[1] Written in 1928.

us that there is no such thing as mind. This is an unprecedented occurrence. Who ever heard of a cobbler saying that there was no such thing as boots, or a tailor maintaining that all men are really naked? Yet that would have been no odder than what physicists and certain psychologists have been doing. To begin with the latter, some of them attempt to reduce everything that seems to be mental activity to an activity of the body. There are, however, various difficulties in the way of reducing mental activity to physical activity. I do not think we can yet say with any assurance whether these difficulties are or are not insuperable. What we can say, on the basis of physics itself, is that what we have hitherto called our body is really an elaborate scientific construction not corresponding to any physical reality. The modern would-be materialist thus finds himself in a curious position, for, while he may with a certain degree of success reduce the activities of the mind to those of the body, he cannot explain away the fact that the body itself is merely a convenient concept invented by the mind. We find ourselves thus going round and round in a circle: mind is an emanation of body, and body is an invention of mind. Evidently this cannot be quite right, and we have to look for something that is neither mind nor body, out of which both can spring.

Let us begin with the body. The plain man thinks that material objects must certainly exist, since they are evident to the senses. Whatever else may be doubted, it is certain that anything you can bump into must be real; this is the plain man's metaphysic. This is all very well, but the physicist comes along and shows that you never bump into anything: even when you run your head against a stone wall, you do not really touch it. When you think you touch a thing, there are certain electrons and protons, forming part of your body, which are attracted and repelled by certain electrons and protons in the thing you think you are touching, but there is no actual contact. The electrons and protons in your body, becoming agitated by nearness to the other electrons and protons are disturbed, and transmit a disturbance along your nerves to the brain; the effect in the brain is what is necessary to your sensation of contact, and by suitable experiments this sensation can be made quite deceptive. The electrons and protons themselves, however, are only a crude first approximation, a way of collecting into a bundle either trains of waves or the statistical probabilities of various different kinds of events. Thus matter has become altogether too ghostly to be used as an adequate stick with which to beat the mind. Matter in motion, which used to seem so unquestionable, turns out to be a concept quite inadequate for the needs of physics.

Nevertheless modern science gives no indication whatever of the existence of the soul or mind as an entity; indeed the reasons for disbelieving in it are of very much the same kind as the reasons for disbelieving in matter. Mind and matter were something like the lion and the unicorn fighting for the crown; the end of the battle is not the victory of one or the other, but the discovery that both are only heraldic inventions. The world consists of events, not of things that endure for a long time and have changing properties. Events can be collected into groups by their causal relations. If the causal relations are of one sort, the resulting group of events may be called a physical object, and if the causal relations are of another sort, the resulting group may be called a mind. Any event that occurs inside a man's head will belong to groups of both kinds; considered as belonging to a group of one kind, it is a constituent of his brain, and considered as belonging to a group of the other kind, it is a constituent of his mind.

Thus both mind and matter are merely convenient ways of organising events. There can be no reason for supposing that either a piece of mind or a piece of matter is immortal. The sun is supposed to be losing matter at the rate of millions of tons a minute. The most essential characteristic of mind is memory, and there is no reason whatever to suppose that the memory associated with a given person survives that person's death. Indeed there is every reason to think the opposite, for memory is clearly connected with a certain kind of brain structure, and since this structure decays at death, there is every reason to suppose that memory also must cease. Although metaphysical materialism cannot be considered true, yet emotionally the world is pretty much the same as it would be if the materialists were in the right. I think the opponents of materialism have always been actuated by two main desires: the first to prove that the mind is immortal, and the second to prove that the ultimate power in the universe is mental rather than physical. In both these respects, I think the materialists were in the right. Our desires, it is true, have considerable power on the earth's surface; the greater part of the land on this planet has a quite different aspect from that which it would have if men had not utilised it to extract food and wealth. But our power is very strictly limited. We cannot at present do anything whatever to the sun or moon or even to the interior of the earth, and there is not the faintest reason to suppose that what happens in regions to which our power does not extend has any mental causes. That is to say, to put the matter in a nutshell, there is no reason to think that except on the earth's surface anything happens because somebody wishes it to happen. And since our power on the earth's surface is entirely dependent upon the supply of energy which the earth derives from the sun, we are necessarily dependent upon the sun, and could hardly realise any of our wishes if the sun grew cold. It is of course rash to dogmatise as to what science may achieve in the future. We may learn to prolong human existence longer than now seems possible, but if there is any truth in modern physics, more particularly in the second law of thermodynamics, we cannot hope that the human race will continue for ever. Some people may find this conclusion gloomy, but if we are honest with ourselves, we shall have to admit that what is going to happen many millions of years hence has no very great emotional interest for us here and now. And science, while it diminishes our cosmic pretensions, enormously increases our terrestrial comfort. That is why, in spite of the horror of the theologians, science has on the whole been tolerated.

INDEX

Routledge Classics
Get inside a great mind

Power
A new social analysis
Bertrand Russell

'Extremely penetrating analysis of human nature in politics.'
Sunday Times

The key to human nature that Marx found in wealth and Freud in sex, Bertrand Russell finds in power. Power, he argues, is man's ultimate goal and is, in its many guises, the single most important element in the development of any society. Written in the late 1930s when Europe was being torn apart by extremist ideologies and the world was on the brink of war, Russell set out to found a 'new science', one which would make sense of the traumatic events of the day and offer an explanation for those that would follow. *Power* is a passionate call for independence of mind and a celebration of the instinctive joy of human life.

0–415–32507–2

History of Western Philosophy
Bertrand Russell

'Should never be out of print.'
The Evening Standard

A dazzlingly ambitious project, *History of Western Philosophy* remains unchallenged to this day as the ultimate introduction to Western philosophy. Providing a sophisticated overview of the ideas that have perplexed people from time immemorial, Russell offers a cogent précis of the subject. Of course this cannot be the only reason it ended up the bestselling philosophy book of the twentieth century. Russell's book was 'long on wit, intelligence and curmudgeonly scepticism', as *The New York Times* noted, and it is this, coupled with the sheer brilliance of its scholarship, that has made Russell's *History Of Western Philosophy* one of the most important philosophical works of all time.

0–415–32505–6

For these and other classic titles from Routledge, visit
www.routledgeclassics.com

Some titles not available in North America

Routledge Classics
Get inside a great mind

Why I am not a Christian
And other essays on religion and related subjects
Bertrand Russell

'Devastating in its use of cold logic.'
The Independent

Considered one of the most blasphemous philosophical documents ever written, and at a time when we have faith schools and wars over religious beliefs, the message contained within *Why I am not a Christian* couldn't be more relevant. If religion provides comfortable responses to the questions that have always beset humankind – why are we here, what is the point of being alive, how ought we to behave – then Russell snatches that comfort away, leaving us instead with other, more troublesome alternatives: responsibility, autonomy, self-awareness. While its tone is playful and frivolous, this book poses tough questions over the nature of religion and belief.

0–415–32510–2

Sceptical Essays
Bertrand Russell

'These propositions may seem mild, yet, if accepted, they would absolutely revolutionise human life.'

With these words Bertrand Russell introduces what is indeed a revolutionary book and today, besieged as we are by the numbing onslaught of twenty-first-century capitalism, Russell's defence of scepticism and independence of mind is as timely as ever. Unwittingly foreseeing the horrors that resulted in the ensuing years from the irrational passions of religious and political beliefs, it is no wonder that *Sceptical Essays* has never been out of print since its first publication in 1928.

0–415–32508–0

For these and other classic titles from Routledge, visit
www.routledgeclassics.com

Routledge Classics
Get inside a great mind

What I Believe
Bertrand Russell

'Bertrand Russell wrote the best English prose of any twentieth-century philosopher.'
Anthony Howard, The Times

Nothing is sacred. Sex, morality, politics, society – all are fair game for Bertrand Russell's acerbic wit and keen eye. With *What I Believe*, first published in 1925, Russell took on organized religion. Along with *Why I Am Not A Christian*, this essay must rank as the most articulate example of Russell's famed atheism. The ideas contained within were and are controversial, contentious and – to the religious – downright blasphemous. More than three-quarters of a century after it was written, its arguments continue to challenge one's faith and assumptions. A remarkable work, it remains the best concise introduction to Russell's thought.

0–415–32509–9

Tractatus Logico-Philosophicus
With an introduction by Bertrand Russell
Ludwig Wittgenstein

'The *Tractatus* is one of the fundamental texts of twentieth-century philosophy – short, bold, cryptic, and remarkable in its power to stir the imagination of philosophers and non-philosophers alike.'
Michael Frayn

Perhaps the most important work of philosophy written in the twentieth century, *Tractatus Logico-Philosophicus* was the only philosophical work that Ludwig Wittgenstein published in his lifetime. He famously summarized the book in the following words: 'What can be said at all can be said clearly; and what we cannot talk about we must pass over in silence.'

0–415–25408–6

For these and other classic titles from Routledge, visit
www.routledgeclassics.com